MISSISSIPPI
currents

MISSISSIPPI
currents

JOURNEYS THROUGH TIME AND A VALLEY

ANDREW H. MALCOLM
PHOTOGRAPHS BY ROGER STRAUS III

William Morrow and Company, Inc.
New York

It is the policy of William Morrow and Company, Inc., and its imprints and affiliates,
recognizing the importance of preserving what has been written, to print the books we
publish on acid-free paper, and we exert our best efforts to that end.

Library of Congress Cataloging-in-Publication Data

Malcolm, Andrew H., 1943–
Mississippi currents : journeys through time and a valley / Andrew H. Malcolm and Roger
Straus III.—1st ed.
p. cm.
ISBN 0-688-11940-9
1. Mississippi River—Description and travel.   2. Mississippi River–Pictorial works.
3. Mississippi River Valley—Description and travel. 4. Mississippi River Valley—Pictorial
works.
I. Straus, Roger. II. Title.
F351.M24 1996
977—dc20
95-41037
CIP
Printed in the United States of America

First Edition

1 2 3 4 5 6 7 8 9 10

BOOK DESIGN BY ERIC BAKER DESIGN

To Connie and Doris

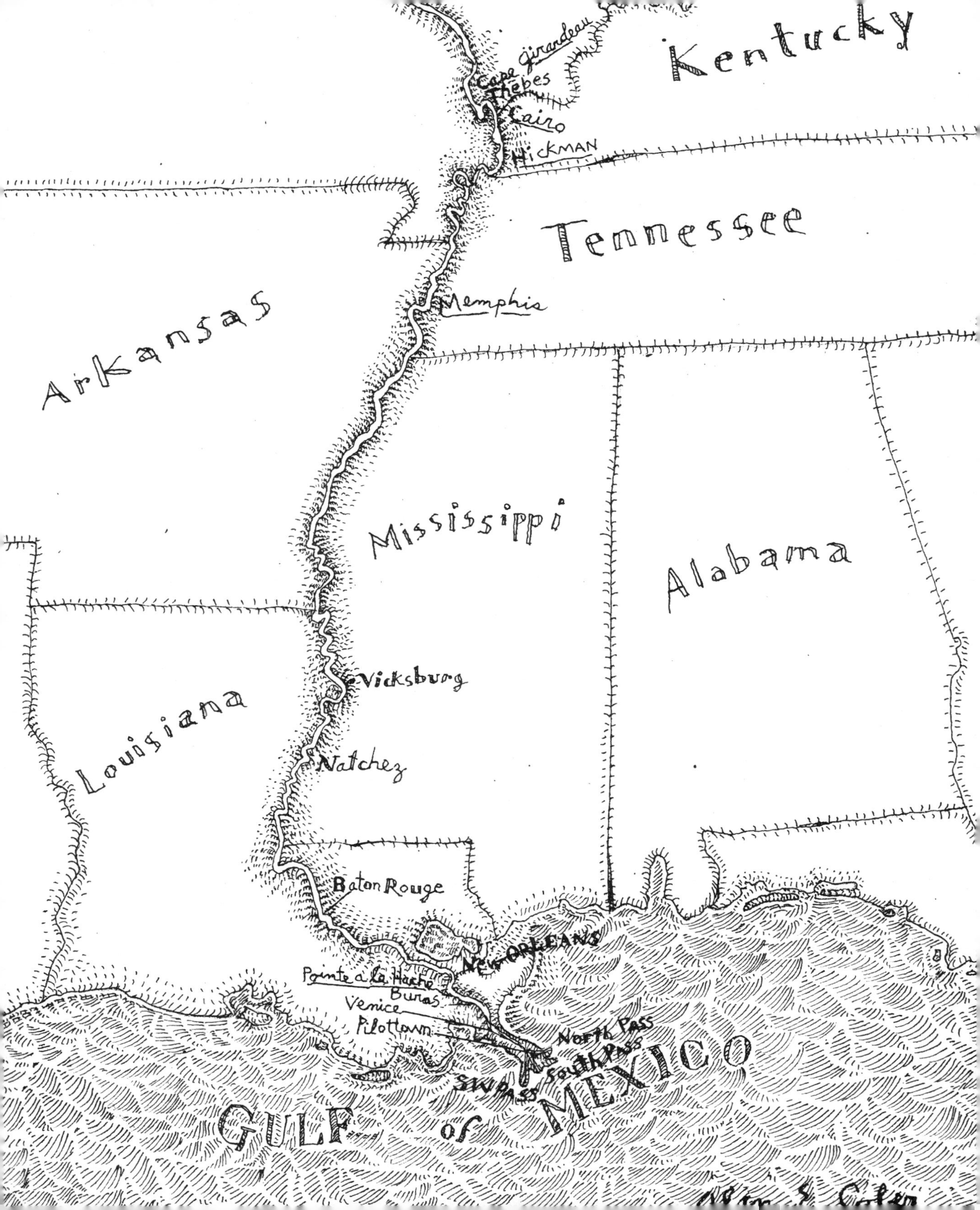

Kentucky
Cape Girardeau
Thebes
Cairo
HICKMAN
Tennessee
Arkansas
Memphis
Mississippi
Alabama
Vicksburg
Louisiana
Natchez
Baton Rouge
NEW ORLEANS
Pointe a la Hache
Buras
Venice
Pilottown
North Pass
South Pass
SW PASS
GULF of MEXICO

FOREWORD

I first saw the Mississippi River from a distance of about 500 miles. I was an elementary school student in rural northeastern Ohio and the Mississippi River was three states away.

But it was also in the children's room of the little library in Hudson, Ohio. There I met Tom Sawyer, Huck Finn, Sid, Aunt Polly, and all the other assorted rascals, pious people, ne'er-do-wells, and scalliwags. I knew nothing in those early days of television about the literary realism that Mr. Twain invented. I knew nothing then—and, frankly, still don't—about virtual reality. But the pages of *Tom Sawyer* and *The Adventures of Huckleberry Finn* were the most compelling reality I could imagine. Every time I read those books, I was right there by the bedroom window giving the secret cat whistle at night and quivering at the thought of entering Injun Joe's cave and lighting out for a secret island in the river.

I, too, carried lucky stones in my pockets and a battered pocketknife. I heard strange noises at night and concocted the most colorful and terrifying explanations for them.

When I first finished those books, I ran out to the barn, gathered up an armload of lumber, and marched a mile or so into the nearby woods to my own secret waterway. No matter it was more of a springtime swamp. It flowed nowhere. And the water, in a very wet year, might stand all of eight inches deep.

With the construction advice of my father, I sawed and nailed and sawed and nailed for many afternoons until—there it was!—my very own river raft.

I jumped on it. It was surrounded by water and trees and rested on the ground. To the eyes of some, that raft never moved one inch from its birth bog. But I can't tell you how many miles we traveled down the Mississippi in my imagination. And the adventures! They would fill another book. River pirates and everything.

So it was with considerable anticipation that some years later I accompanied my parents on a long rail journey from Chicago to Memphis. There I was tucked into a foldaway bed in my own compartment with a sink that actually folded into the wall. I had no idea some sinks did that. That false revelation later prompted a bathroom experiment back home that created the sudden need for a plumber.

I slept soundly on those starched sheets until a noticeable slowing of the train awoke me after midnight. I lifted the window shade to peek out. That night, I had seen the wonders of Philadelphia and the Empire State Building and the Cleveland Browns. And I had met Satchel Paige and longed to know a little girl named Judy Homchis. But my juvenile mind was not prepared for the magical sight that was passing just outside my window.

In honor of my visit, the Mississippi River had escaped its banks and flooded everything in sight, everything except the railroad trestle we now crept along. The bright moonlight showed me trees standing tall in the water. The tops of some houses—just the roofs—could be seen at times. But nothing else. Nothing but water. Now, I had bounced through a Saturday fishing trip on Lake Erie in my life. I had thought that was a lot of water.

I watched the rampant Mississippi River out that train compartment window until I could no longer keep my eyes open. It was no coincidence that when it came time as a young adult to seek my first newspaper job, I headed straight for Memphis. There I began learning how much I did not know. But I also endeared myself to one of those grizzled old newsroom editors who always wore a fedora indoors. You see, he had a little wooden fishing boat. He needed help maintaining it. And I needed rides in the warm summer sun on the Mississippi River.

I spent twenty-six years then with *The New York Times* reporting, writing, and eventually editing news articles, and even writing a column for an inspirational spell. Much of the time was spent wandering in Asia and the length and breadth of North America. Somehow, from time to time, I would always find a journalistic excuse to get myself on or along the Mississippi River.

Some people revere the ocean, which is nice and big and all. But for me oceans just sit there. Rivers go places and do things, none more so than the Mississippi.

This book is a joint journey with Roger Straus III, the renowned photographer, through a river valley and a period of time. The river is always there as a theme. The people come to its banks from all walks of life for all kinds of reasons. They come to play and stay. They come to work and fish and live. They come to feel small and inspired. They come to be comforted. They come to study this natural power that the Indians revered, too. That's what we explore here, all the many ways that people affect the river and are, in turn, affected by it.

This river, in a very real way, is a living symbol of the historic, powerful region it drains. The Heartland has turned out much of the nation's food and values; its politics and leaders, including three of the last five presidents; its culture and inventions. It has turned out the steel plow that changed the way the world farms, the airplane that changed the shape of travel, the skyscraper that changed the shape of cities, the assembly line that changed the shape and scale of industrial production, the fountain pen that made the quill obsolete and changed communications, and the suburbs that changed the way working Americans lived and emptied the inner cities they fled.

The same region that is home to the tornado and the twelve-mile-tall thunderstorm also produced the world's first controlled nuclear reaction. The Mississippi Valley harbors no small thoughts. It has spawned populism, half the presidents since the Civil War, and so many other Americans who have affected the way we live and think—from Abraham Lincoln, who poled down the Mississippi, and Daniel Boone, who hunted along it, to Ulysses Grant and Andrew Jackson, who fought along it, and Samuel Clemens, who lived, worked, and wrote on it. The same region has produced Edgar Lee Masters, Carl Sandburg, Ernest Hemingway, Theodore Dreiser, James Farrell, and Walt Disney, all liberators of a nation's fears and fantasies.

And while we explore this river and this valley, we also end up exploring ourselves and our country, our priorities and passions, and how they have changed in recent times, perhaps for the better. Through pictures and words we'll wander past some of the richest countryside and poorest people in the United States, through placid pastures with herds of Holsteins and into communities that think to erect DUCK XING signs to protect their nonhuman neighbors. It is an unpredictable journey we are taking. But that's not a bad thing if we allow more such serendipity into our lives. Who knows where it might lead?

Roger Straus has spent much of his life in Manhattan, where they believe the Passaic River joins the Gowanus Canal to form the Atlantic Ocean. But he has also wandered most of the world's continents with his weighty shoulder bags of cameras, lenses, and film and brought back insightful images for us to enjoy and ponder.

As for me, I live on the Missouri River now. There's probably no connection. I'm just the group leader, always curious about why things are as they are, who that is over there, and what's around the next bend. Someday, I'm very sure, I will peek around yet another of those bends in the river. And there he'll be, Huck himself, with a spare straw hat and some words of advice about that motionless raft I built so many years and miles ago.

I hope you'll join us on this journey through a place and a time.

Andrew H. Malcolm
Helena, Montana
May 1996

ACKNOWLEDGMENTS

The author wishes to thank everyone involved in the work on this book. It is impossible to list them all by name here. However, they each appear in their own story within this literary journey through a time and a place.

They gave, thanklessly until now, of their time and minds to answer my relentless questions, to show me their lives, and to share their knowledge of the river. Many times, I am sure, these questions seemed strange at best. Well, we all have our own distinctive fingerprint. And we all have our own way of traveling. This was mine, and I thank each of them profusely now for sharing their wisdom, their time, their memories, and their lives with me—and now with countless other readers.

I must also thank Connie, my wife, editor, and pal, for her professional suggestions and insights and her personal suggestions and insights. Her understandings and encouragements made a project of this scale, in the end, definitely doable.

Finally, I must express my deepest appreciation to my partner and pal in this journey across America. We have done this joint journey once before along the length and all three lanes of U.S. 1 from Canada to Key West. I stop the car. And he takes pictures. And takes pictures. And takes pictures. And takes pictures.

My admiration for his keen photographic eye is outmatched only by my genuine personal appreciation for his endless patience with me. That may even flow deeper than the river's standard nine-foot channel.

Andrew H. Malcolm
Helena, Montana

If you're feeling cranky, take my advice and spend some time on or along the Mississippi River. Not only is it one of nature's really impressive waterways, but also it is peopled by an extraordinary cast. I thank everyone we met during our travels for their generosity and good humor. In particular, I wish to thank the brave residents of the Quad Cities. I visited the Quad Cities on three occasions. The last trip was during the terrible flood of 1993. Even confronting harrowing circumstances, these remarkable citizens were unfailingly kind and helpful. You have my sincere thanks and admiration.

It seems that both Andy and I have live-in editors. I don't know how it works at Casa Malcolm, but at my place it goes something like this. I show Doris something I'm working on, say a portion of this book. She says, "That's great, but what if you did so and so." I immediately disagree, pointing out the perfection of my efforts. The next morning I realize, with horror, she's right. I make the changes and am quietly grateful. So I thank Doris for improving this book and more so for blessing my life.

Most of all, I'd like to thank my good luck, and one of my great pieces of good fortune was stumbling across Andrew H. Malcolm. To have a partner you admire is satisfying. To have a partner who becomes a dear friend is even better, and then to be able to wander this diverse country together is good luck indeed.

Roger Straus III
City Island, New York

CONTENTS

Sunrise, Lake Itasca, Minnesota

Morning fog, Lake Bemidji, Minnesota

The source of the Mississippi River, Lake Itasca, Minnesota

Angler's Beach Resort, Cass Lake, Minnesota

Angler's Beach Resort, Cass Lake, Minnesota

8

The railroad station, Red Wing, Minnesota

The railroad station, Red Wing, Minnesota

Ice fishing, Red Wing, Minnesota

Lake Pepin, Minnesota

Lake Potosi, Wisconsin

THE BEGINNING

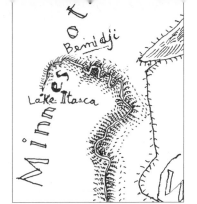

It began nearly two million years ago with the delicate descent of a single snowflake drifting through gray skies to settle on the soil, silent and unseen.

The earth had been cooling for centuries by then, and was near the beginning of the last of several waves of global refrigeration that had helped kill the dinosaurs and alter continental coastlines and climates. The last one would promote prehistoric migrations of humans and animals, and otherwise starkly change the face of this solar system's most dynamic planet. That snowflake fell somewhere in what would become Canada's Northwest Territories. It landed on marshy ground that was once the soft, fecund bottom of a shallow sea sprawling over much of North America. By that gray, unmarked day, however, the ocean floor had been frozen into a frigid rigidity that has yet to lose its grip beneath some modern-day moss.

That snowflake was followed, over scores of centuries, by trillions upon trillions upon trillions of others, in numbers beyond counting. Without the warming liberation of annual springs, these crystals of moisture piled one upon the other higher and higher and still higher until, in some places, they stood two miles thick. The immense pressures of their weight turned the snow below from powdery drifts of windblown white into vast sheets of slippery blue ice that shifted and groaned and began to slither across the continent's face like gargantuan serpents.

Sometimes the advancing icy tongues of these creeping glaciers moved eight inches in a year. Sometimes eight feet. Sometimes not at all. Sometimes these frozen masses collided and, for some uncertain, unnoted centuries, contended for icy dominance of a path, scouring out an unusually wide valley during their graceful, seemingly motionless geologic pas de deux.

Sometimes they forged ahead, unhindered, with an elemental, inexorable power. Everything gave way before them, forests, hills, even great lakes, which were gouged deeper by this grinding mass of jumbled rock and debris shoved ahead in slow-motion chaos.

When the glaciers receded, as they sometimes did for a geological instant, they left behind lines of stones, bones, and boulders as momentary monuments to their farthest advance. Long Island, New York, is one of them. So are the Great Lakes. Beneath these sprawling ice masses, ten thousand feet below the halfhearted sun's meek rays, the monstrous frozen fields deposited the fine-ground remnants of defunct sea bottoms and immense boulders they had consumed along their route. In some places these glacial droppings were one hundred fifty feet deep.

They still are.

Soon, in 150,000 years or so, the ice sheets returned, snowflake by snowflake, inch by inch, ton by ton to grind another chapter onto the unpopulated landscape, to erase the geologic trails of past advances, and to shoulder their shifting burden even farther south. So great were these masses of frozen might in capturing and holding in frigid suspension the globe's supply of moisture that all the oceans fell 300 feet in depth, moving shorelines many miles.

But then, on a sunny day perhaps twenty-five thousand springs ago, the latest warming chapter opened. Snowflake by snowflake the glaciers began to melt. The tiny drops of moisture fell to the warming ground, unnoted still, to be followed over time by trillions and trillions of others.

At first the water soaked only adjacent soil. But that became saturated. So the water began to trickle this way and that through the rocks and fresh dirt, following the downward path of least resistance as dictated by the unseen grasp of gravity. One by one these trickles mingled, first forming rivulets and then small streams, which paralleled and merged with others to form larger streams and small rivers and then larger and larger waterways in a shifting, serendipitous journey to an undetermined natural destination by an uninhabited shoreline at the bottom of this continent.

From the very beginning, this powerful, stubborn, sprawling, destructive, life-giving river dominated and dictated the lives in its regions. In fact, the history of humans on earth is largely the history of rivers and the cultures that developed along these sources of life, food, and transportation. Where the streams flowed straight, the surging waterways lifted specks of soil and carved dots of sand from the underlying sheets of stone and carried them along in a sometimes somnolent, sometimes turbulent murkiness that deepened the channel even more. It took four hundred thousand years and several geologic chapters for the ice, the water, and the tumbling silt to carve the gargantuan gully that now runs from Minneapolis to southern Missouri. That gully created first a prehistoric wildlife migration route that survives to this day, as do the legions of human hunters who migrate there, too, every autumn, now armed with pump-action shotguns instead of stone clubs. Still chugging by nearby are the boats, driven by oil not steam, that push the barges that drain the Heartland of its agricultural bounty year-round.

Where the river wandered sleepily in endless eddies of brown, slowing itself to irrigate most efficiently but still seeking the easiest route across the gently rolling countryside, the waters ate away at their outside banks and deposited their bounty of soil along the inside banks, creating prairies, and ever-wider arcs of irrigated fertility. Until, over time in its own time, each arc became too long, too slow, and too full, setting off another of those pendulum swings of change that reassure country people and pass right by city folks, who live by more precise human schedules.

The river then simply sliced a shortcut through the countryside, cutting off the aging loops and turning the old bows into new, comma-shaped lakes. They imprisoned the river's creatures in suddenly still waters whose remnants by the hundreds line the Mississippi River Valley to this day like so many discarded punctuation marks littering the land.

Thus fed, but untamed, unbroken, and uninhabited by humans, these adjacent prairies proceeded to develop a coordinated bounty of natural riches. They had the deep-rooted grasses that held the soil in place, waiting. They had the weather that fed the lakes and streams that still meandered back and forth. They had the winds that whipped the lightning fires to and fro that burned off the trees and grasses that left the nitrogen-rich ash to feed the soil's fertility for another day. They had the forests clustered around the springs and the rivers. And they had the little creatures that fed the large creatures that eventually attracted the humans, who would for reasons of economics, politics, happenstance, coincidence, and greed, change it all, thinking they knew better.

But always the prairies had that central artery of water that flowed down the long spine of the continent every day of every year collecting the waters that came to flow, the animals that came to drink, and the humans who came to kill.

With the extinction of the continental glaciers, some thousand centuries ago, North America's runoffs formed over time their own particular pattern of merger—little streams to larger ones and larger ones to the main river, which often merges with other main stems to move on at its own pace inexorably, downhill, toward the sea in cycles that know no end. To the eyes of presumptive human engineers, who always prefer straight lines as tidy as those within their neat notebooks, this tortuous network seems grossly inefficient; to Nature, which does not operate by fickle fiscal appropriations, the same system had, unaided, irrigated and replenished the most land with the least water for eons. And, anyway, what's the hurry?

Eventually, more than two hundred fifty of these major rivers, each individually awesome in its own right and each with its own sprawling system of contributing brooks, streams, and rivers, joined to form a massive water-way that the Indians called Messipe, "the father of running waters." The white men mispronounced it, and as members of Congress and engineers often do when they encounter natural things that awe, they set out to conquer this elemental force, thinking they could.

But you never conquer rivers this powerful. Nowadays, at the last river lighthouse, out on the Delta beyond sight of the North American continent and just across from a small herd of cattle foraging in windblown litter and the fallen mud of the Midwest, more than two million cubic feet of these combined waters—one hundred twenty-four million pounds—roll by every single second. So vast is this volume at times that this river flows on and on for hundreds of miles through the Gulf of Mexico, intact as a freshwater river within a salty sea.

Suspended on this miles-wide tide every year are hundreds of thousands of tons of man-made cargo, grains mostly, and petroleum products, lugged away on blocks-long strings of barges pushed by blunt-nosed boats named for distant women who do not likely smell of diesel. Navigating the narrow channel through the nights and days, in fair weather and foul, with a strict protocol that predates Mark Twain, these powerful craft with brass propellers taller than a car pass within yards of preoccupied river communities, unnoted and unnoting as they move up and down the Heartland's watery back street past the porches and garages of more than seven million Americans.

The crafts' masters chatter routinely on radios that give familiar voices to faceless boats. These commercial commuters, their decks perpetually pounding to the explosive rhythms of the internal combustions occurring below, carry their own populations of characters. And they portage their own floating cultures of traditions, hearty meals, jokes and jealousies, running card games, flu epidemics, well-worn video libraries—few of them rated G— and hardworking, rough-hewn crews of itinerant inland maritimers in frayed flannel who chew tobacco and speak Louisiana with an American accent.

The same vast river also transports, silently and sadly, the natural refuse of a continent's rural society: sodden logs, unlucky cows or pigs, even entire fallen trees; plus all the detritus of a careless industrial society: garbage, sewage, plastic bags, and chemicals, sometimes even a human body or two. Suspended also in the same wondrous and disgusting tide, drawn annually from thirty-one states and destined to disappear in international waters, are three hundred fifty million cubic yards of dirt, enough soil to cover nearly nine hundred square miles of land three feet deep.

At the top of this jagged, meandering, ever-moving network of water and suspended cargo, far above a city called Minneapolis, sits a lonely, once-wild woods in a plot that now requires protection. Enclosed in that woods, surrounded by the spindly pine stalks characteristic of such northern forests so short of warm, summer days, is a small lake, largely indistinguishable from thousands of others gouged out of the landscape by those prehistoric leviathans of ice.

This lake, perpetually patrolled by bugs, was not visited by white men until nearly one hundred sixty-five years ago when they came for an afternoon in borrowed canoes, seeking something they could not define. The questing people from away still come today, in Winnebagos, in minivans, and in rented sedans. They come on snowmobiles, skis, and bicycles. They wear wrinkled shorts and shirts or, come winter, Arctic space suits with ample zippers, pockets, and shiny-shielded helmets with colorful corporate logos proclaiming allegiance to oils and racing teams. They carry Kodaks across the ice-crusted snow to record their historic moment by the carved wooden sign, often forgetting to include the water itself in the photo frame. Still, they come to visit this nondescript lake for a few hours for reasons they're unable to explain, if they try, although many toss in coins in incoherent tribute.

This lake collects the waters of a half dozen nameless local streams, including one silently seeping up from below. From its northern end, by thickets of dead brush, this wild, pristine pond, named by a prideful nineteenth-century explorer for an irrelevant Latin acronym that would make any pedant proud, gives off barely a minor gurgle at the start. There it frees an ankle-deep stream of crystal-clear liquid to tumble over a line of well-worn rocks. That marks the beginning of a wandering, eclectic, yet vital months-long working journey of nearly twelve and a half million feet through the Heartland descending a quarter mile in altitude along the country's economic spine to the Gulf of Mexico.

Sometimes the water moves along beneath sunny skies, sometimes black clouds, and sometimes gray ice. And all the while it grows larger and larger, touching, shaping, nurturing, enhancing, and sometimes taking or ruining the lives of millions and the economy of an entire region, whose residents never thought they were in the way of anything larger than a summer thunderstorm.

From this pedestrian source, initially headed in the wrong direction, springs the mighty Mississippi River. And almost as many stories as there once were fallen snowflakes.

There is Jack Katzenmeyer, who presides with country pride over that little lake and the woods around it. There is Donald Gustafson, who runs the general store that provides the food and postcards that fuel the visitors. There is Charles Ansardi, a Southern cowhand on foot who drives some cows along the rich, green banks and hates snakes. There is Tom Pokrefke, who sits on an aluminum platform using a computer and confetti to trace the currents and to ponder the hidden inner workings of the rivers within his river. There is Michael Duncan, who punches a clock before midnight and dreams of the freedom he feels out there on the water on his weekends. And there is Bert Morris, who lives and works on the water around the clock and dreams of the freedom he feels when he leaves his dieseled domain.

There is Earl Hingle, who after all these years still crosses the river to reach the town he owns where no one lives but dozens of Democrats still vote. There is Dale Fox, who runs the ferry that still crosses the river in endless, mile-long cycles of air-conditioned shifts. There is Davey Johnson, who loves the heat and flying through it at high speeds and low levels, as he did so many times so many years ago elsewhere when others shot at him. There is Harry Jones, who would rather not be there but didn't bring up the subject when his wife didn't ask. There is Leland Olivier, whose hoses and pumps still seek to shape the river bottom he's never seen. There is Jim Hearon, a lonesome old man who donned a secret identity to infect river passersby with his love for literacy.

There is Berlin Moreau, who mines the river's water for living creatures; an entire town that mines the memory of Mark Twain; George Matthews, who mines the sympathies of river buffs; John Hall and his cats, who mine the river's scenery; and Malcolm Burt, who mines the wallets of those who come down to the river to see and rediscover that modern human need to buy one of those sartorial postcards, the T-shirt. There are Nathan Beucke and Libby Minor, who come down to the river to be seen pretending so that others can feel freer doing the same. There is Diane Eyink, who comes because of Jerry and the childhood memories he's shared; Thelma Foutch, who comes to wait; and Pete Mueller, who comes to explore the possibilities of chance, according to design.

There is Jim Slavens, who brings his customers from abroad for the excitement they share out there romping on the famous water beyond the painted lines and rigid rules of city life. There is Shelly Bennett, who came down from the mountains to see where the water was going that she had watched flow by for a childhood. There is Wayne Stroupe, who likes living where so many died. And there is Mike Bray, who brings Keith for the solace they share there, away from her.

The Mississippi River is a vital economic route and a stirring symbol for the mid-American psyche, simultaneously inspiring and frightening, practical and romantic, one of those immense, contradictory natural forces that makes humans feel so small yet reassured: We are important, though not as important as city dwellers think.

And always there is the water, the endless brown water that predictably comes, never stops, and usually goes with a soothing seasonal rhythm that calms people as long as it continues, making men and women go slower too and ponder unusual things like what's around the next bend.

But before the first bend, there are the beginning and Jack Katzenmeyer, Dorothy's son, who lives atop the top and watches with the astute eye of a park ranger, the only one to live year-round at the source of the great river.

THE TOP

The Mississippi River heads west for its first three hundred feet before ducking to the right beneath a wooden footbridge and doubling back east through the protected woods past clumps of wild grasses on narrow banks that tempt hikers to leap across, if their mail-order boots are waterproof. Those first hundred yards are among the few straight stretches as the juvenile waterway finds its way across the isolated, lumpy flatlands of rural Minnesota through lakes full of fish and mosquitoes, woods lush with deer and birds, and towns with more pickups and dogs than sedans and neckties.

Jack Katzenmeyer is coming up on fifty now, all of those years spent within a few miles of the beginning. He came as a young flunky, doing official state maintenance work in a park that had gotten along just fine maintaining itself for countless millennia before the arrival of the lumberjacks and then, soon after, the legislators.

Now, of course, since he works for a government and governments thrive on social stratification to fit the various bins on the bureaucrats' desks, Jack is called a park technician. He's really a ranger, overseeing the campgrounds where nearly 100,000 people annually vie to pay four dollars to sleep on the ground beneath the stars that seem more numerous in Minnesota on those northern nights after the sun finally sets and the insects finish their first feeding.

"This is a very special place for a very large number of people," he says. So large, in fact, that the campgrounds—indeed, the entire park—are literally crawling with people from Memorial Day to Labor Day. SORRY—WOODS ARE FULL. Even the wary beavers have constructed second sets of summer homes to get away from the crush of urban humans fleeing their own winter residences.

There is something mildly pathetic about Americans' drive to have their parks, those carefully defined areas of presumed pristineness that let us all feel less guilty about raping the land everywhere else. Because we've preserved some tidy blocs as museums of nature, it's okay to subdivide the others. As long as we keep the lines as straight as the ones television weather forecasters feel compelled to draw for us around every state and province on their satellite photos of North America.

So we pile into the family car to flee the fumes and crowds of our urban metropolises while transporting the same fumes and crowds to a carefully controlled plot of park that lets us feel we are somehow recharging our Jeffersonian ideals. The parking lots are jammed. The well-trodden park paths appear paved, though they're not. The garbage cans are overflowing by Saturday night. And there's always some group that brought along a cassette mountain of electronic noise to share with everyone within stereo range.

On a summer day, the 54.7 square miles of Lake Itasca State Park will contain one thousand people in its campgrounds, another two hundred–plus in its lodges, thousands of other day visitors, and one hundred thirty employees, including those in the headwaters gift shop, which specializes in virtually every imaginable headwaters souvenir—from T-shirts and one-size-fitzall caps from Korea to thermometers, place mats, and refrigerator magnets. Small souvenirs (from the French verb *souvenir* meaning "to spend way too much for a trinket to remember an otherwise forgettable time") are big business in modern America. But more on that as we drift downriver to Memphis and Malcolm Burt, who never met a passerby who didn't need his product.

Itasca is Minnesota's busiest state park, every year attracting a half million visitors, more than the entire population of Wyoming. That's a lot of posed snapshots, twenty-five-cent postcards, and wishes made by the water. "We do not remove the coins," says the veteran ranger. "Somehow they find their way out of here safely."

But making a reservation to sleep on the ground is not the only activity in Ranger Jack's park. There's lots more for the mobs to do once they buy their tickets from a small town–friendly Ellen MacNeil at the North Gate. There's hiking if you have the correct mail-order shoes, fishing if you have a license, bicycling if you follow the signs, swimming if your blood is still thick by July, boating if you don't go too fast, and, of course, picnicking if you can find a parking space and then get to the tables in time (and survive the pesty patrols of yellowjackets).

Natural northern woods can be somewhat scruffy affairs with legions of skinny trees competing for sun in the long days of the short summers. But Itasca is a park. That means wildfires are officially prohibited, at least for a while. So the trees get larger. So, too, of course, do the tons of dried brush waiting for the irregular conflagrations and resulting ash that put refuse to reuse. But the carefully written rules of modern parks also require that they be protected from themselves; so fences go up to protect infant trees not from the grasp of wild children but from the indiscriminate jaws of an overpopulation of hungry deer who can't have anything bad happen to them. That's because they live, overprotected, in a park where Man's version of Nature is imposed so that humans can get a taste of the wild, although by confining it for this purpose, it isn't really as wild as everyone likes to think.

It was Jacob Brower's good idea in 1890 to create Minnesota's first state park so as to deny some land to the lumber barons hacking their way across North America, a strange idea on frontiers but one that won the approval of the state legislature, if only by a single vote. Brower, who was named the first park's first commissioner, predicted that Itasca would "become easily accessible and of great value as a public resort," a remarkably accurate assessment made without the assistance of an environmental impact statement or consultants with an unusually comfortable hourly rate. Even a century ago, the struggle between developers and preservationists, between jobs and scenery, was itself developing well.

The Indians had been puzzled for two centuries by the bearded white men who regularly passed through, desperately seeking the beginning of the big river, as if they were in a race that mattered. The Indians had always reasoned that the whole river, which they variously called Mischipi, Messipi, and Meschasipi, was important, not just its head, that life itself was much like an endless, untamed river with countless additions and subtractions along the route, and too much of one over time meant too little of another. These natives are the same folks who harvested only one or two eggs from a wild bird's nest, reasoning that was their share and to take more would eventually threaten to unbalance the larger flow of life. As an integral but not controlling part of Nature, the nomadic natives saw concepts like ownership as foreign and irrelevant technicalities as long as everyone along the water's path shared access to its bounties. How could any civilization survive without sharing? Who would dare to presume ownership of, let alone control of, an elemental, spiritual force as large as The River? Who could have a pride so overpowering as to attach individuals' names to geographical locations?

Hernando de Soto had reached only the lower Mississippi in 1541, although he got there some seven decades before anyone stepped on Plymouth Rock. (That got him the honor of having a now-defunct line of cars named for him.) In 1673, Father Jacques Marquette and Louis Jolliet traveled downstream. (They got a couple of cities named after them.) Seven years later, Robert Cavelier didn't bother to travel beyond the mouth of the Mississippi before claiming the entire drainage for France. Around 1800, David Thompson, one of the least known and most adventurous explorers of North America, passed near Bemidji and identified Turtle Lake as the source.

Lewis Cass sought the source (and got another lake named for him). So did priests: Father Joseph Nicollet went looking for the headwaters (and got a downtown Minneapolis mall named for him). Reporters waving fraudulent maps and trappers with piles of pelts joined the hunt, even ambitious Army officers; Zebulon Pike was in on the search (but he had to settle for a peak in Colorado).

Ostensibly, the searches for the Mississippi's source were driven by the Treaty of Paris, which, in 1783, established the river as the northwest boundary of the United States. By implication, everything west of there did not belong to that teenage nation. It fell to Henry Rowe Schoolcraft, a pedant, and his practical guide, Ozawindib, to make the definitive discovery, on July 13, 1832, during an expedition to inspect fur forts and minister to the medical needs of Indians. After what seemed like days of canoeing, weeks of portaging through knee-deep mud, and swatting at "voracious long-billed and dyspeptic musketoes," they reached the water called Omushkos or Lac La Biche, both meaning Elk Lake. After one afternoon's paddling around the modest body of water, the modest Latin-literate professor pronounced the lake the real source and renamed it Itasca (from *veritas caput* or "true head"). Although several streams merge to form that lake, Schoolcraft reasoned from his canoe that the Mississippi River did not exist until that water left the lake on its journey to the Gulf.

Canoes were the primary mode of early transport on the watery highway. The Indians were interested in speed and maneuverability and fashioned each canoe from one long piece of birch bark stripped from a riverbank tree. They used the canoes for hunting, fishing, and even as working platforms for women harvesting wild rice, a religious and dietary staple. For good luck, each brave carried the tail of a woodchuck, a superstition modified to a rabbit's foot by the white man, who had small pockets.

These latecomers to mid-American river life also modified the canoe for reasons of—are you ready?—profit; the bigger the canoe, the more furs per trip. Bigger is better. That's the hollow North American philosophy that explains many modern problems, including New York City. Big canoes were a tradition to be continued later by the owners of nineteenth-century steamboats and twentieth-century barges. A trading canoe could be thirty-five feet long and six feet wide, capable of carrying five dozen ninety-pound packs of animal skins, one thousand pounds of provisions, plus eight men, each with a knapsack. This four tons of commerce could make four miles an hour on calm water, more with the current.

Ten miles an hour is the summertime speed limit now on Lake Itasca, which means no waterskiing. In winter the surface traffic can move somewhat more swiftly when the Upper Mississippi seems locked in a rigid coat of cold that forces even the large logging trucks to wear sheets of vinyl for radiator protection against the mean Minnesota windchill. By night the Mississippi's headwaters are largely silent, save for that minor gurgling around the hundred pumpkin-sized rocks spanning the waterway's start, the eerie, irregular groans of trees bending to a cold breeze, and the howls of coyotes or wolves. Above, the big black sky, dotted with countless specks of twinkling light, seems so much larger than its blue daytime counterpart.

At these times the pristine headwaters can seem devoid of life. Far from it, of course. Sitting at the rough conjunction of the pine forest dipping down from the north, the hardwood forest rising from the south and east, and the prairies sprawling one thousand miles to the west, Itasca is home to a rich variety of wildlife and plant life, from the yellow orchid and delicate trillium that announce springtime to bunchberry, aster, and lady's slipper, Minnesota's state flower. Black bears are common, along with raccoons, skunks, porcupines, and an overpopulation of white-tailed deer, who know a good source of food when they find one. So, too, do the coyotes, now ubiquitous across the Midwest even in new suburbs, and the timber wolves moving back down from Canada even before a free trade agreement.

Bald eagles hang around the headwaters, by the open water at least, as do ospreys and the common loon, whose uncommon song adds such mystery to summer evenings on the water. The raccoons scurry industriously along the streambeds and in and out of the campground garbage cans, while the area's beavers, like many of the humans who hunt them with cameras, build two homes: one on the main streambeds and another, more isolated, farther upstream out of range.

Thousands of ducks breed at the river's source—the bobbing mallards, the ever-alert golden eyes, and buffleheads, as well as the colorful mergansers, who dive so methodically and swim so powerfully out of sight for their fish dinners. Not to mention the redheaded woodpeckers, real-life cousins of the cartoon Woody, who patrol the pines for boring pests, and the two-legged birders with binoculars, who come to quietly catalog all the winged wonders.

By midwinter the lake ice is upwards of three feet thick, strong enough to support six-packs of pickup trucks portaging little wooden windbreaks and parka-clad fisherpersons with perhaps more patience than sense. The ice grips the lake for five full months. But still they come, by the thousands.

"No, Lenny! I told you. That's the largest coin I have." They come in all seasons from all continents (FOOTPATH TO HEADWATERS) by bus, by car, by van and motorcycle, by snowmobile and bicycle, even on skis or foot, to march a few hundred yards down a slushy, graveled path (450 FEET TO HEADWATERS) past a wooden unisex outhouse (TOILET) to the understated beginning of the mythical Mississippi at the jumbled pile of rocks that silently invites sneakered feet to step out on them.

After twenty years the Hennen family came back. Jack and Mary brought Jamie the first time on a camping trip. All three have long since outgrown camping, or at least their aging backs have. But they wanted to revisit that place and their memory. And so on one wind-free February weekend, they drove five hours from their suburban Minneapolis home just to stand there again, together.

"This place hasn't changed!" Jack proclaimed with the conviction of a juror relieved at the verdict. "It just has not changed. Think about how much water has gone over those rocks after all these years."

"Frankly," said Jamie, "I don't remember much about it."

"It's nicer in the winter," added Mary. "Not so many people."

The wet cold does discourage dawdling. But still two dozen people stood around briefly, skipping stones, taking snapshots, and waving silently while smiling, as videocameras cause people to do.

Although the clothes of summer visitors are skimpier and the pace of the tourists is slower (often, wading visitors simply stop midstream, causing a pedestrian traffic jam atop the prehistoric rocks), the larger fair-weather crowds are not all that different. There are the first-timers like the

Riesterer family—Fred, Karen, Paul, and Michael—out of St. Andrews, Manitoba. "Well, of course, everyone has heard of the Mississippi," said Fred.

There are the repeat visitors like Ray Iaquinto, a retired diesel mechanic, and his grandson, Jeremy. "Fifty years ago," said Ray, "we used to swim in this river down close to The Cities right by Earl Brown's farm. We had a rope on a tree limb, you know? We'd swing out and drop in. You wouldn't see anyone all day there. And I remember you could see the river bottom clear as day back then."

And there are the repeat visitors with newcomers like the Jimeno family from Austin, Texas—Julie, Manuel, Erik, and Andrew. "I was here years ago," said Julie. "I sort of dragged the family this time, to see if it'd changed. C'mon, Andrew, wade with me. Oh, come on. Look, it's only knee-deep. You know, there's hidden treasure in this river. Look! There's a quarter!" Within seconds, Andrew is wading.

The Hennens opt not to wade on that February afternoon. But they do use the river often near home. Jack's independent gas station has prospered in recent years. So virtually every warm weekend they take their sixteen-foot boat with the seventy-horsepower motor out on the river for a drifting dinner below St. Paul. Being on the river lets them feel free of the pressures of daily life, even though the waterway runs right through so many lives. And barreling across the river, or simply drifting lazily, gives the Hennens a sense of open space they no longer have in their backyard, especially with the fence.

Suddenly the silence of the woods is shattered by the bratting roar of six snowmobiles arriving from South Dakota in an urban hurry. It's The Drift Busters out of Aberdeen. Dressed like Martians with space-cadet shields screening their faces, these time travelers seem oblivious to the noise in their snowy wake. They don't mind being noticed. And they are more than ready to stretch their legs and pose for snapshots by the headwaters sign.

"Well," says one, "where's the river?"

Kathy Dummer-Stolte can spot the foreign tourists immediately: They're the ones carrying a Mark Twain book. And they don't seem fazed at all by the ungrand beginning of the grandest river in North America.

Ms. Dummer-Stolte is the headwaters park naturalist. She grew up on a hog farm in southern Minnesota and migrated to northern Minnesota for college, then to New England, where she found her neighbors colder than the climate. So she returned to the upper Midwest. "People come up and say, 'Where are the headwaters?' And I say, 'This is it.' It's rather stunning to see the big beast as a polite little stream."

Her whole working life has been to help get the headwaters heading off to a good start and to explain its seemingly simple workings around an endless series of summer campfires to urban residents more likely to think of water as flowing from a faucet. Still, they come to see it, in such growing numbers that the park felt the need to protect the infant river's crumbling banks by building a winding wooden boardwalk along the first few twists and turns. Riverbanks are made for crumbling, of course. But already within the first one hundred feet of the Mississippi's source, mankind is trying to change nature. Overall, that is a gargantuan multibillion dollar effort that began more than one hundred fifty years ago and has yet to end, despite convincing irregular evidence, in the form of floods, that continental rivers draining one and a quarter million square miles across thirty-one states and two Canadian provinces do not like to be confined on their serendipitous, inexorable way to the sea.

Although there can often seem to be a more pressing need for Ms. Dummer-Stolte to explain the behavior of these visitors than of the river, probably no river reality could ever live up to the epic literary flow portrayed in Twain's wry writings. They are required reading in many overseas English classes, especially in Australia, Japan, and Germany, compelling proof of the Danube Factor.

Now the Danube Factor may best be described as the peculiar mental phenomenon that causes so many non-Austrians to imagine every living soul along that European river's romantic banks as forever waltzing. Just as it is impossible for non-Austrians to imagine a Viennese who doesn't wear a swishing silk gown or a tuxedo to the no-doubt daily balls at the palace, it is beyond the belief of foreign readers of Mark Twain that the Mississippi might be anything other than a vast, powerful waterway awash in mud, exotic catfish, and the most compelling cast of roguish characters ever drawn in words and delivered by steamboat. There is something about rivers as constantly changing theatrical stages that inevitably involve their audiences, like a graceful Oriental garden or lady's garment that incite the imagination not by what they reveal, but by what they silently suggest.

The visitors looking for roguish characters stop in all the time at the Gustafsons' General Store. What they find are the Gustafsons—Don and Deloris—and Dorothy Katzenmeyer, Ranger Jack's mom, who is postmistress for the outgoing flood of cards and the incoming trickle of bills and letters that works its way up and down the twenty-seven miles from the larger post office in Park Rapids. This trio comprises one half the full-time population of Lake Itasca, MN 55460.

They see the visitors—and the souvenirs—come and go. The most popular souvenir, of course, is the headwaters postcard, the colored twenty-five-cent one that shows the sign describing the river's 1,475-foot drop from Lake Itasca to the Gulf of Mexico. In fact, that's one of the largest sellers for Dick Shalow's NMN Inc., one of the nation's numerous, hustling little companies producing regional tourist effluvia—the postcards, pennants, key chains, mugs, T-shirts, sweatshirts, beer can holders, and elongated, neon-colored back scratchers whose manufacturers employ many people elsewhere. The economic dictates of the modern tourist business, not to mention the innermost workings of free trade, require that Dick's headwaters photo be shipped to Australia for postcard printing and then returned in bundles by sea, train, and truck to Lake Itasca for sale, postage, and individual shipment back out by sea, train, truck, and plane to places like Germany, Japan, and Australia. In the souvenir business, these well-traveled personalized pronouncements of exotic travel, random reminiscences that are the material descendants of the Muslim mementos portaged home by returning Crusaders, make as much sense as the feathered Native-American headdresses shipped in from Sri Lanka.

Not all headwaters visitors are transitory tourists, however. Many are regulars. They come not so much to see the famous flow's humble beginnings, but to share the place regularly with kin. On the surface, the town might seem an inauspicious place to share—St. Catherine's Church, the nearby park gate, the general store–post office that also serves as a Mobil gas station, complete with the familiar, if outdated, flying horse symbol, and that's it. For one hundred years the little store has stood there, peddling the eclectic collection of convenience store goods that people traditionally tend to forget when they're packing for their camping trip or cruising the grocery store aisles in town—the toothpaste, toilet paper, canned soup, boxed noodles, cold remedy, propane bottle, antidiarrheal kind of store.

But, *ahh*, from another corner of the old, winter-weary structure comes the fragrance of Deloris's special chili, her bacon, and her family-famous buttermilk pancakes from Grandma Lindgren's own recipe. They are served along with the standard diner menu in the Backroom Cafe, so named because it is in the general store's back room. "It's a good business," says Don. "We can make a living."

Deloris grew up on a small farm just north of town, one of countless minor family farm operations across the region that helped stock the country's reservoir of values and gave their owners a priceless sense of satisfaction, working the land and animals, but never gave them quite enough cash to get along on one job. So Deloris's father also did occasional construction work.

The children helped out in the barn, of course; their favorite chore was skimming the cream off the silvery metal milk cans before the truck from Shevlin made its regular pickup rounds. Naturally, some of the cream just happened to spill into a barn bowl or two, which explains the sudden, early morning appearance of every cat in kittendom. The rest of the cream and butter went into the towers of buttermilk pancakes that fueled the family so many mornings at first light after the day's first round of chores.

Regular rhythms are essential elements of rural life—the seasons, the storms, the snow, the sun, the births and the deaths, the gawky calves, the vigilant mothers, the grumpy bulls, the family dogs, the profusely procreative cats patrolling the barn, and the news from elsewhere of all the strife that seemed so far away before satellite dishes cropped up in so many backyards like expensive dandelions. Life seemed family-focused in those days, more tied to hands-on relationships that required—and received—constant tending, like an active August garden.

As sure as the frost came by mid-September, every year—on July Fourth, in fact—the Lindgren clan would gather in the park by the headwaters for a family reunion. The date was a given. The daughters with their families would just count on coming home then. The men, who still worked the land, and their sons, who had jobs and developing lives in towns now, would be off work that day, also with their families. They wore their good jeans and clean caps on that day, and probably cleaned up their language a bit, too, the way men do in mixed company and around their parents.

They'd start gathering naturally near the water, like springtime sparrows coming home to roost, pretty soon after church, if it was a Sunday. First, the men and the boys who wanted to act like men would drag together a dozen or more of the park's weathered wooden picnic tables before heading off for a softball game. The women in this pre-Tupperware era began unloading and placing the huge unmatched glass bowls of their covered food contributions on the checkered tablecloths waving gently in a light summer breeze. Tons of potato salad, chicken, scalloped potatoes, wieners, potato chips, cold cuts, homemade breads and mustards, and, yes, there they were, an entire table of fresh-baked cakes and pies that attracted the little boys like pesky yellowjackets sensing the snacks. Every youngster had to sneak a fingerful of frosting, which tasted all that much better because it was allegedly forbidden. But the worst anyone got was an empty scolding. What Lindgren woman in her right mind in those days would object to relatives who couldn't wait to taste her desserts? In fact, truth be told, as in every family, each one of the women individually kept very close track of the consumption of her confections as the afternoon wore on. In a properly considerate world, there would be no leftovers of cake or cookies, although, of course, there always were, although, of course, no one in the families ever said anything, although, of course, the women never failed to take note themselves.

Members had their assigned jobs from previous years—the fire starters for the hot dogs, the potato salad makers, the cake bakers, the scalloped potato makers, and the lazy, lovable few who drifted from table to table sneaking snacks before the blessing. Card games would likely break out, and games of tag. And even if it wasn't quite warm enough, some youngsters would inevitably strip down and go skinny-dipping and scream joyously about the cold water.

At some point, of course, Deloris took her turn sitting down next to Granny Lindgren, who quietly presided like some Hawaiian matriarch, though, another truth be told, she could no longer remember all the names of all the grandchildren and great-grandchildren and great-great-grandchildren running around.

Pretty soon, however, it was time to eat the food, which was blessed first, of course, by the son-in-law who was a minister and then consumed in a delicious marathon of munching spiced with a stream of family stories, a kind of verbal annual yearbook. The women were the ones who kept track of the new babies and new husbands and wives, and the illnesses and even a few deaths, from the previous year and over the years. They're the ones who preserved the oral histories while their men sort of listened, please pass the salad, between por-

tions, and, anyway, the guys' stories were tied more to work or sports, especially the Twins or Vikings. Those were safer subjects, it seemed. Women talk about themselves and each other. Men talk about their teams.

Soon, of course, the combination of food and hot sun sent many away from the tables to snooze a while on a soft bed of needles beneath the headwaters park's thick old pines that had been observing July Fourths without notice since long before there was a dream of independence, let alone a country or a Lindgren clan to celebrate it.

The reunions went on like this, so comfortable and reassuring in their rhythmic predictability, for nearly a half century. Until that first July Fourth after Granny Lindgren's passing. For a good number of years there didn't seem much point, without the Granny connection, to assembling a gang of dissimilar in-laws and cousins, now suburbanized, whose regular playmates and Little Leagues were back home.

The park had changed somewhat, too, by then. It had fewer picnic tables. Or maybe it was just more people. So it had more rules to be enforced by more rangers who, unlike Jack Katzenmeyer, didn't live in these parts year-round. And more litter, since no one seemed to bring food in glass containers anymore; so many more things in society had become disposable by then, even relationships. And visitors could no longer simply pull off the road anywhere to park, though the pavement was wider. Those new rules again. More fences had gone up to steer the traffic and the strollers, many of whom wore headsets to keep out the woodlands' silence. The scattered tables were anchored to the ground now for reasons that seemed unremarkable to vacationers from a city.

But Deloris Gustafson got an idea one recent winter. Maybe it's something old-fashioned that just happens genetically when you become a great-grandma. Or maybe July Fourth had just seemed too empty of family for too many years when people celebrated it by sleeping in and washing the car and then perhaps watching the fireworks from some distant city on TV because the small towns had gotten so they couldn't really afford much of a fireworks show, what with the budget cuts and teachers' strikes and tax revolts and all. But Deloris got the idea that a whole bunch of family would gather together on that day for a picnic in the park over by the Mississippi's historic headwaters.

She knew probably most of the families would end up bringing a bucket of commercial fried chicken and a store-bought pie because both the husband and wife had had to work late at the office the previous day. But maybe even if the folks weren't initially all that eager to drive several hours to meet their relatives, perhaps being at the start of this famous river for a sunny afternoon would prove an attraction, even without any multimillion-dollar theme park rides. Deloris had visions of a friendly mob of relatives coming to know each other better through that gathering and sharing food and stories and celebrating their shared family-ness along with their shared citizenship and independence in a familiar forest where so many others before had shared that same holiday at the start of something so big and so famous, the Mississippi River.

So over the course of several wintry evenings she wrote up a bunch of invitations and next morning, one by one, dropped them in the slot over in the corner where Dorothy Katzenmeyer runs her post office. The letters soon left by truck back down the road to Park Rapids and then on out to the other world. And while Deloris waited to hear back from the relatives she might no longer recognize, she talked enthusiastically about the happy scene she envisioned that coming summer.

The tables would be laden with food and the barbecues smoking up hot dogs. Maybe a softball game would break out. Some dogs, newly freed from the back of their families' minivans, would be running and jumping around. The women would bring each other up to date on the doings of recent years in their family branch. And maybe some sweaty youngsters would go swimming. Then, everybody would eat together and compliment the cooks and, most important of all, share the tables with people who shared their bloodline.

Soon, of course, the combination of food and hot sun would send many away from the tables to snooze a while on a soft bed of needles beneath the headwaters park's thick old pines that had been observing July Fourths without notice since long before there was a dream of independence, let alone a country or a Lindgren clan to celebrate it.

And the river would flow on.

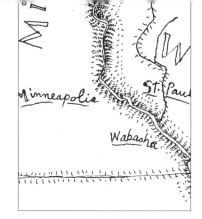

THE JOURNEY

The Mississippi River breaks out of the northern woods like a youngster freed for recess. Never mind that it heads in the wrong direction. It is still young and clean and small enough to wander across dozens of private farms, where people think of it more as a sturdy stream than as the powerful precursor of the world's third longest river, which it becomes several states from its source.

For eighty miles the juvenile flow meanders north and east, as if seeking its way back to where, more than twenty-five thousand years ago, the last wave of founding glaciers spawned the river systems that now irrigate North America. Only fifty of these ice masses survive now in the lower forty-eight states, all of them still in suspended animation and safely tucked within the confines of another park aptly named Glacier in faraway Montana, where the Mississippi's big sister, the Missouri, rises for its own long journey to join the journey to the sea.

Over the centuries, the glaciers growled down over much of North America in the temperate ebbs and chilled flows of the Ice Ages, sometimes extending as far south as the southern tip of Illinois. So massive were these oceans of ice that they scraped clean whole regions, leaving few physical traces of their geologic doings for later generations of Ph.D. candidates. So big were these ice masses that they shaped the climates to their own frigid needs for thousands of years, constantly cooling them by the few degrees sufficient to alter what could grow for hundreds of miles.

Studying old plants and other revealing minutiae, scientists can tell that the climate in the Mississippi's neighborhood was noticeably colder than today. Endless stands of pines and larch sprawled across the South then, much as they still do today across the river's northern beginnings.

The Mississippi River changes course every thousand years or so, its massive burden of water and soil carrying within itself both the silty end of one waterway and the watery impetus to find new lower, shorter roads to the sea, even if it has to work for a few centuries at opening the way. In many places the river is still actually following the fundamental, intertwined scars of the scouring glacier generations. The glaciers, too, always sought the lowest point. They carved out the Great Lakes, granite canyons, and whole new systems of rivers, which thanks to the newly hewn valleys and channels, began to flow south, instead of north as before.

Fed by the vast volumes of the melting ice packs, these new rushing waterways in turn excavated their own way through the land in a miles-wide series of braided southbound streams that merged come spring into a massive flow ten times the size of springtime flows today. Not accidentally, during these overflow seasons the river's waters and associated winds delivered, minute grain by minute grain over the eons, millions of tons of silt from the river's excavations up north to replenish the temporarily sodden riverside fields down south and to construct, quietly beneath the waves, a vast extension of the North American continent, the Mississippi Delta. Amazingly, the diverse streams did all this by themselves, without a single congressional appropriation.

At drier times, the new systems of parallel rivers pursued their own independent paths to the Gulf. They all flowed quickly in those days because the mass of water tied up in northern ice was so great that sea level back then was far below today's, making the riverbeds steeper. Over the centuries, that gradient has lessened below as the sea level and the surrounding land mass rose. In many places near the mouth now, the Mississippi River falls only a few inches per mile. In Minnesota, however, the river is still carving away at the land. It has, for instance, eaten away about one hundred feet of dirt and gravel by the Minneapolis–St. Paul airport. In fact, more than 640 of the Mississippi's total 1,475-foot fall occurs within Minnesota.

Besides steepening the river's run, the lowered sea level of the last Ice Age also exposed much of the bottom of the Bering Strait, issuing a geographic invitation to some Asian bands and the animals they hunted to wander over and become the first inhabitants of North America. Ultimately, chased by winter and some other warlike groups, they moved down across the length and breadth of this more hospitable continent, where they were drawn to water.

Water has always been the magnet for life in this world, be it wild, plant, or human life, biblical or more modern Gomorrahs. Where water flows, life goes. Which explains the Oregon Trail following the lines of willows and cottonwoods wandering across the prairies as well as the location of cities everywhere from New York to Paris, from London to Tokyo and back to St. Petersburg and Venice, where the streets are rivers. The path of Mississippi water and life also explains the location of Minneapolis–St. Paul, St. Louis, Memphis, and New Orleans, which basically floats in place on a massive river bog. And although each succession of those marauding glaciers erased the trails of its predecessors, farther south scientists can track the nomadic animal and human cultures that tracked each other along the river. The stony spear points, the high-banked ambush sites, the white bones, the black charcoal, they are all there to tell the tales of life and death to the informed eyes of later generations of hunters with shovels, brushes, notebooks, tweezers, and minds educated to imagine the struggles of humans wearing animal skins and exotic creatures who never knew of the Endangered Species Act.

The mastodons are gone. But other species of wildlife, driven by instinct and interior genetic maps, still follow the Mississippi and its tributaries in their semiannual migrations up and down the land. So, too, come the modern-day hunters, driven less by hunger now than by instinct and habit, in their rubber boots, camouflage clothes, and four-wheel drives. From aluminum boats and the rented blinds of their killing clubs, they blast away at the sky with pieces of lethal lead and dispatch dogs for the wet work of fetching the fallen fowl.

Other people come to capture photographs, even to write books, or just to witness the wondrous squadrons of ducks and geese making their noisy way, reassuringly, down ancestral paths. And still other seasonal travelers come to see the colorful death throes of the leaves on the deciduous trees that grow there, now that the glacier-free climates have warmed five to ten degrees.

Serving river visitors is how John Hall makes his living in Wabasha, Minnesota, marketing scenery, nostalgia, and caramel rolls, not necessarily in that order.

He owns Anderson House (MINNESOTA'S OLDEST OPERATING HOTEL SINCE 1856). It started as Hurd House, a hotel riverboat stop and winter home away from home for riverboat men and downbound loggers. That was back before frequent flier miles, when seasons ruled men's lives and work and the frozen river awarded its employees a few months off every year. Even before central heating, Hurd House was a pretty fancy place among the twelve or thirteen hotels that served the many visitors who came and left Wabasha's waterfront and flour mill on business or for pleasure. Hurd House was probably the first establishment in town to have cords in every room connected to numbered bells downstairs, which, when rung, summoned, naturally enough, the bellboys to take a food order or portage some leather luggage down to the dock.

The river stayed, of course, though the work and the workers on it changed. With the coming of the railroad and the paved highways with their pell-mell pace to everywhere, the drifting flatboats disappeared, nevermore to make their one-way downbound journeys to New Orleans with farm goods and young men like Abraham Lincoln seeking adventure aboard some logs lashed together. Gone, too, were most of the steamboats with their huge rushing paddle wheels, their twin smokestacks, their fragile hulls, and the busy filigree of wood and metal that bespoke luxury to nineteenth-century eyes. They gave way to a compact corps of fume-spewing, dieseled towboats that make romance harder to conjure. The towboats muscle their cumbersome strings of laden barges up and down the river nonstop, in company with a few ersatz passenger steamboats that try to capture an old-fashioned era—for a new-fashioned price.

These working boats don't stop much anymore in Wabasha and other similar river communities along the

Mississippi. Time is money. And stopping costs money. Now, even groceries are delivered to the through-boats on the fly by local tugboats summoned out to mid-river by radio calls for supplies or fresh crews. Although they never move exactly fast, the towboats might slow even more to deliver or collect another barge or two, likely loaded with grain to feed people far away who never heard of the Midwest or Wabasha. And the boats certainly don't emit bubbly calliope music anymore as they come and go at all hours, according to a business schedule set by money and computers.

Hurd House was not alone in feeling the economic impact of such changes. The hotel's regular visitors no longer came regularly. Those there tended to stay, like water in a backwater eddy. Not much work elsewhere for their age and skills anyway. In the 1890s, Hurd House became Anderson House when Ida Anderson—Grandma Anderson to everyone—bought it. Under the homespun management of Grandma and her determined descendant family, the hotel became more of a long-term residence for aging men who were likely less interested in dressing for dinner than being left alone on some long hallway of hermits. By 1976, the residents were paying thirteen dollars a week for their rooms, or two dollars a night, which was about one dollar too much, according to some memories.

Then along came John Hall, now at the half-century mark in his life. A much younger John had washed dishes at Anderson House. But being young, he had headed off up the river for the bright lights and busy-ness of the big city. He worked for Sheraton Hotels in Minneapolis, Chicago, and Los Angeles. But Grandma Anderson's great-grandson had an idea. He wasn't the first or last to have this idea, given the developing plethora of bed-and-breakfast places across this land of leisure.

That's the key: Leisure. There's more of it nowadays, too much of it, if you listen to some of the well-informed social observers of ennui, who track the national consumption of things like beer, wine, Prozac, cocaine, violent movies, TV, and theme parks. With shorter work weeks, longer vacations, and more two-income, one-child families, there's a limit to how many times even a well-rested husband during one of the overlapping sports seasons can steer the TV remote control box around forty-plus cable channels. And there is a limit, too, to the glitzy—and costly—appeals of Fifth Avenue, Michigan Avenue, or Rodeo Drive.

So where would a small-town great-grandson of an innkeeper look for the commercial pendulum to swing back to? John Hall's mind returned to the wonders of a stable, backwater riverfront community and his family's Anderson House on the Mississippi River, where the sun still glints on the slow-moving water, and people still notice. It's amazing how hard people work in faraway places so they can return someday to where they came from, like salmon in another river. Hall did not anticipate the high costs and interest rates of bringing a well-used, fifty-one-room structure up to the standards of nearly twenty-first-century fire codes. But a private entrepreneurial dream, combined with some big-time hospitality experience, an abundance of home cooking, and a roomful of affectionate felines, can be a very powerful force.

So is nostalgia, that inexplicable human sentiment that makes old things seem deliciously new. It's the familiarity factor. Fashion designers have refined it quite well. So have the purveyors of golden oldies. But nostalgia also carries potential for the travel industry.

John Hall with employee, Anderson House, Wabasha, Minnesota

Once, loading towel-wrapped warm bricks in a bed was a winter evening's chore. Now, it's a novelty. Once, most every meal was fresh-baked and home-cooked. Not anymore. Unless you're staying at Anderson House, where every room is different, where the furniture is antique, the beds are made of black walnut, and the shoes of guests are shined overnight. The cookie jar stands chock-full on the front desk, mustard plasters await guests wid a code en da hed, and the bathtub is just down the hall, sitting regally high on its lion's paw feet, ready to envelope a reclining guest in hot water, clear above the shoulders.

"We do things exactly as they did in the 1920s," says Mr. Hall. That's back when rooms had keys, not cards, and customers had names, not PINs. To be sure, Anderson House rooms do have color televisions because, besides colorful leaves and curious sightseers, Midwestern autumns bring football. One suite has a whirlpool bath. All rooms have Christmas trees come December. And all rooms also have air-conditioning; enthusiasm for nostalgia—or anything—has a way of wilting in Minnesota's summer humidity.

But there are no 800 numbers, no phones flashing urgent messages, and—are you ready for this?—no microwave cooking and heating of instant consumables with invisible rays. That's because Grandma Anderson was actually a Pennsylvania Hoffman. Lancaster County, to be exact. That's chicken and dumplings country, homemade noodles, Dutch apple, southern pecan, sour cream raisin, lemon cloud, and double Dutch fudge pies. Plump doughnuts.

The cats of Anderson House, Wabasha, Minnesota

Prime rib, cheese-stuffed, bacon-wrapped sausages, roast loin of pork with stuffing, and roast pheasant and ham potpie, too. Thank God for cooks who work the same kitchen for two decades or longer and then compile a series of Anderson House cookbooks (available at the front desk).

But, wait! There is also breakfast, including a diverse bread tray (Irish barnbrack, blueberry streusel, limpa, orange, cherry, banana, pumpkin, and cranberry breads, among countless others). And then, It arrives. A caramel roll. Plate-sized. Fresh-baked. From scratch. At dawn. Caramel. Brown sugar. Corn syrup. Butter. Served warm. Two hundred times a day, one is served. Hey, the locals may not stay there much. But they're not dumb. They know a fantastic coffee break meal when they see one. In fact, hungry Sunday morning sleepyheads without a reservation may well be without a meal.

Mr. Hall does not put all his loaves in one basket. He also operates a brisk bus touring business, carting loads of excursionists to Arizona and Florida in the winter, New England and Nova Scotia in autumn, and Alaska in the summer. But the hotel could never survive financially without outsiders. Leaf-peepers. Skiers. Retired couples. Traveling salespersons. River buffs. Antique shoppers. They know about hotel chains, computerized reservations systems, loud lounge bands playing frantic songs for empty dance floors, plush-carpeted, cookie-cutter rooms with knee-banging desks, and in-room cable TV systems with adult movies no one admits to watching.

To survive without all those wonders, all the world's Anderson Houses must find a market niche. For Mr. Hall, that's nostalgia—and cats. You see, besides reserving a room, Anderson House guests can also reserve a cat. There's a form for that: the Cat Reservation Form. Take your pick of a furry snuggle partner for the night—Aloysius, Tiger, Ginger, Bess, Fred, Pepper, Chester. Nineteen in all. No extra charge. The felines live there anyway, in a modified hotel room overseen by Catie Taubel, the cat woman.

In the cat dorm each has its own carpeted shelf, an immense supply of toys and perches, and a picture window to monitor street traffic below. In return for putting up with this, all they have to do is sleep on—or in—a different guest bed every night, allow their ears to be scratched, and feign liking the leftover pheasant from room service. The overnight pals are delivered to guest rooms at 5 P.M. with their standard cat dinner and a pan of kitty litter. Mr. Hall buys that stuff a half ton at a time and three thousand pounds of cat food per year. The veterinarian also likes Anderson House.

Maids collect the cats come morning and return them to the dorm, except for Muffie, who has wandering rights and parades up and down the front sidewalk all day like a living billboard willing to accept the attention of and scraps from patrons of the hotel's small sidewalk café.

Like many communities sometimes feeling bypassed by opportunity, Wabasha has sought to attract visitors and their wallets by developing itself as a destination for tourists, some place to spend disposable leisure time and disposable income, with no pollution save a passing array of telltale regional accents. It has chosen the path of more traditional outdoor activities—river excursions, skiing (cross-country and downhill), iceboating, icefishing, ice-skating, snowmobiling, sleigh rides and sightseeing (nearby is the birthplace of Laura Ingalls Wilder, whose book *Little House on the Prairie* garnered fame for her dead self and loads of money for others through a medium she never saw).

Then there is America's traditional indoor sport, shopping—for souvenirs, clothes, antiques, ice creams, wines, and cheeses (Wisconsin is just across the river), often in that peculiar new variety of American shoppe that spells its name in British and an epidemic of apostrophes, as in Soaps 'n' Spices, Cookies 'n' Cakes, Buttons 'n' Bows, Crafts 'n' Things, Shirts 'n' Shorts, and Cards 'n' Stuff.

Ken Hottenstein, Potosi, Wisconsin

Many customers come 'n' go by boat, as befits a waterfront town that had a riverway long before a highway. Anderson House even runs a shuttle bus to the marinas, where the well-heeled tie up their colorful leisure machines for a day or a dinner onshore. Kenneth Hottenstein and Pete see them coming and going all the time. The engines of some are strong enough to drive airplanes. They go by at a crazy pace, sometimes fifty-five miles an hour on water that might be doing four. The engines' roars no doubt scatter the unseen reptiles below. The large, powerful wakes, as impertinent as the weekend captains standing proudly at the wheels of their fiberglass dreams, charge several feet up the landing, which explains why Kenneth and Pete seem to sit a little far from the water's edge.

Kenneth and Pete just watch silently together. Not much else they can do. Kenneth has a little folding stool he brings down to the water a few miles from his home on the Wisconsin side of the Mississippi. Kenneth sits on the stool as if the landing were his front porch and the river his main street. And Pete, quite possibly the Mississippi's crabbiest terrier, lies underneath in his master's shade.

Kenneth's father was a carpenter, though he had his own horse and buggy. Weekends, he'd take his boy down to the river to fish. They'd sit here together and wonder where the water came from and where it was going and where the darned fish were that day. Kenneth's grandfather was in the Civil War, also the California Gold Rush, if you believe the stories. The stories Grandpa would tell! Kenneth doesn't remember them now. But he remembers they were really something.

Kenneth used to make tractors in a factory downriver. He did that for more years than he can remember. But they don't make so many American tractors anymore. So Kenneth took the early retirement deal. The factory closed down soon after. It wasn't the only factory to wither in these parts, the victim of changing tastes, methods, Asian robots, and corporations that were worth more as dead deductions than as live manufacturing facilities on the financial chessboards of wheeling and dealing conglomerates. That was a lot of fishing trips ago.

They don't seem to make as many fish anymore either. But Kenneth drives slowly down to the landing several times a week now. He fishes from ten until twelve and then two until five, unless they're biting good. He and a few other early retirees like Bill Horner, who's over eighty.

Bill wasn't eager for retirement, either. But one day the highway department men came. Bill knew they were trouble right off; he saw the suits and ties and the ominous briefcases. Real people don't carry briefcases on social calls. And they don't order the cheapest draft and then not drink it. The briefcases said the state wanted to widen the road. Bill's tavern was built in the days of the Model T, back before TV and air-conditioning kept people at home, back when people went for a drive, not to go anywhere but just for the novelty of driving faster than a horse away from city crowds. Now the appearance of the highway men said that Bill's life—his cozy career with its soothing familiarity, the worn stools, the dusty, lighted Hamm's beer sign, and the bar well-worn by the elbows and the sad stories of so many Happy Hours—now all this was in the way of the future.

The cars go faster now, of course, like everything else, which explains all the backward baseball caps. Fleeing from the crowds, the automobilists created their own new crowds everywhere they went. So the vehicles need more concrete to move along, naturally. The drivers aren't looking for places to stop anymore, unless it's one of those window-

less malls with more acres for parking than shopping. People are too busy to pause much anyway, too many things to do in their leisure time, too much purpose. And they're usually late, it seems. So Bill's tavern, along with Kenneth's job, had to disappear. Sign here, please. That's progress along the river.

Bill Hoover, Potosi, Wisconsin

They sit a few fishing poles apart on the landing nowadays in the summer sun that warms the stones too much for Pete's feet. They toss their lines in a short ways offshore, each using his own special bait. Kenneth's is chicken livers and worms. Bill's is classified.

They say they're waiting for fish—cat-

fish, hopefully, though nothing anywhere near the size of the fish in the old days before the dam went in. Legend says the old days saw 120-pound catfish. Or maybe a batch of bluegills. It's a meal anyway, as long as you don't wonder what the fish themselves have been eating. And a fish is one of the few things a man can earn these days that isn't taxed somehow. Hattie Horner doesn't like to fish. But she does like to eat the occasional results. And Bill likes the way his wife fusses over him and his fish when he returns home with a few in his battered pail.

"And it's a peaceful way to pass the time," says Bill. "That's what I like about it. You know, away from all the noise and talk you don't agree with. It doesn't matter if you get anything." Sometimes Bill's son, Orrin, comes along with his dad to not catch much. They pass the time together, the banks of large rivers being great for time-passing. They sit together there, apart a ways, not talking much unless it's sports, which is safest. Bill says Orrin would have come today, too. But he's got tickets to Saturday's game. And you know how wives are if you spend two days with the guys so close together.

A brief breeze riffles the Mississippi's surface.

Kenneth and Bill sit there most days and hold the ends of their lines trailing in the water, helplessly hoping for luck to strike, and thinking. Sometimes they exchange what can pass for conversation among men.

"Water looks to come up some."

Ten minutes pass.

"Thought I had one there."

Two minutes pass.

"What you say?"

"I said it might be too hot today."

Five minutes pass.

"It was hotter the other day when I caught two."

Some barges pass.

"Before the dam, there was trees all over out there."

The feeble barge wakes reach shore, weakly lapping at the gravel.

"Pete, sit still, for Pete's sake."

Three minutes pass.

"How big was that one?"

Silence.

"I figure four pounds."

Five minutes pass.

"I caught a forty-pounder out here one time. Actually, it was thirty-nine pounds, but I still call it forty. Sounds better."

Four minutes pass.

"That was back in '55. I had a seven and a half horsepower motor in those days. They came out in '55."

Two minutes pass.

"That's how I remember."

In 1955, Jim Slavens was thirteen and falling deeply in love—with the Mississippi. He lived in Davenport, Iowa. He still does. "I have been all over the world," Jim says, "and dollar for dollar, the quality of life is highest right here." People seem to stay along the river or, if they leave, eventually they return for good. Mud gets in your veins, river lovers say, smiling.

Jim's dad was in real estate. He loved the river, too; most people do, until the first time they're flooded out.

Then they see the waterway more like a drunken dad; it can be foul and frightening, but it's the only one you've got. So there's an elemental tie that lingers longer, no matter what. It's much harder to divorce dads or rivers, which explains why their offspring keep coming back regardless of the damage.

Jim's dad built a small apartment building overlooking the river. He installed his family there, too. The Mississippi views are better from the Davenport side; they're not blocked by the artificially high horizon of the levees that line the riverbanks in most places where the governing generation remembers previous springtimes.

The countless episodes within the long hours of teendom have a way of taking forever to pass by. And then later, in memory, those seven years merge into a single mass. But Jim remembers vividly sitting on the grass and watching the river, how it moved by so slowly and inexorably, how its color and demeanor changed with the clouds. If it rained, he watched from the living room window. The river was so big and so powerful, sometimes so moody, but always so very large and strong. And a little scary because of that size and strength and because it is always moving on, always, no matter what, like life. Jim read Mark Twain's books with amazement. The river was just as alive in them as it was just outside the living room window. More people now, perhaps, with definitely different values. But the river seemed the same. That reassures a lot of people, like some emotional mooring, in an age when everything else is changing.

Sometimes, if Jim begged enough, his mother would pack a picnic dinner and the family would eat on the front lawn right by the river, just to be in its passing presence. "The river," Jim still says, "becomes absolutely a vital part of your life." People walked by the river. People sat by the river. They drank beer by the river. They swam in the river and fished there. Some died in the river, if they weren't careful or lucky. They fell in love by the river. And they quite possibly did other things by the river.

All his free time, Jim Slavens invested along and in the Mississippi River. Come summer, he'd go swimming in it almost daily. It wasn't very clean. In fact, it was downright filthy. He'd come home for dinner, pretty much browned up with mud. "Go wash out your mouth," his mother would say. So he would.

At fifteen, Jim made an announcement to the family:

I need a boat. His father bought one for the family, thinking he would use it sometimes for business. But he always had to check with his son. Most nights Jim had it out on the water. He was too young to drive a car. But there he was, with no need of a license, at the helm of a speedboat roaring up and down one of the world's greatest waterways, turning here and there and over there, wherever he wanted. No one could tell him what to do. He relished the sense of freedom and control, no tethers anywhere, no boundaries to life at that moment, save the distant riverbanks of the mundane land-bound world. The wind blew by, the brown and whitish wake billowed up behind, the open water lay ahead, for as far as Jim could see or imagine. God, it was good! And fun.

It still is. James Slavens is slightly over fifty now. He is president of an important bank. And he's got a handsome personal investment portfolio. He also has a one-million-dollar souvenir in shredded dollar bills in a Federal Reserve bottle on his desk. Jim's brother is his bank partner. Jim's mother is on the board, too. Jim's got three sons that he raised in his house on the river. More important, Jim Slavens has two boats.

He's got a "little" runabout with more horsepower than a major stable. The eighteen-footer could outrun a lot of vehicles on an interstate—and probably take them in a drag race, too. Move the silver throttle to Full and that little runabout stands on its stern like a nitro-fueled funny car. It roars like one, too. You'd better be sitting down then. Or you'll be swimming off the stern right quick. That baby's got cushioned seats, a cooler, and a serious sound system that Jim turns up high to match the wattage of his smile. He might even sing along loudly, if the day has been good. Or even if it hasn't. Standing there at the controls, leaning forward against the surge of his speed, confronting the elements and sensing through his rubber-soled shoes the rumble of the precisely programmed explosions beneath the deck, Jim can feel the music and the wind blowing strong in his happy face.

"I said," he said, "it's full-fledged freedom out here, isn't it? No stop signs. No lanes. You decide where you want to go. Watch this."

At more sedate times, Jim will take out his other toy, a thirty-seven-footer called *The River Banker*, which he ties up in the family's slip, No. 88, at the Lindsey Park Boat Club. His boats are in the water right around Eastertime and get little rest before the middle of football season.

At least four nights a week, with friends or alone, Jim is out there on the water cruising, sometimes drifting, sometimes thinking, always doing. "The river has always helped me keep a sense of perspective," he says. "It's timeless, you know. It was here long before we were here. And it'll be here long after we're gone, like the mountains. Only the river moves. There's a life and a peacefulness in that."

The river is not bad for business either. Davenport is one of the so-called Quad Cities, along with Bettendorf on the Iowa side, and on the southern Illinois side, Rock Island, Moline, and East Moline (yes, that's five, but the Quint Cities sounds funny). Some three hundred fifty thousand people live in and around these river communities. Forty percent of them live on the wrong side of the Mississippi, meaning they must commute across it every workday, which makes for three very crowded bridges twice a day. But in the 1980s, suddenly, 14 percent of the Quad Cities' workers were without jobs. It was the unemployment office that was crowded.

These communities rose up originally because of their location on the water. The Weyerhausers floated their long log trains down from the north to mill here. Encircled by immense timbers chained together like floating fences, these drifting masses of fallen trees could stretch six or eight blocks long. International Harvester came with J. I. Case, John Deere, Montgomery Elevator, Caterpillar, their suppliers, and countless other manufacturers.

They all sent their goods and the massive harvests of food and grain from the surrounding countryside out to the world, likely on the river. Those were good times, well-paid jobs with security and benefits. Clutching battered lunch pails, sons followed fathers into the sprawling factories that throbbed with productivity and confidence that the future would continue to produce predictable prosperity—and abundant overtime—instead of lengthening lists of dislocated workers and families. That was before wives became wage earners, too.

But grain embargoes, international politics and competition, the inexorable rationalization of the Rust Belt, changing mores, and fear took their toll on these cities and their peoples in recent times.

Jim Slavens saw all that. He tried to help where and when he could, not wringing his hands for long over the end of old jobs but working very hard to help stimulate new ones. There were challenging times. But every few years Jim could still buy a new runabout. "It's time," he would say.

Even the worst flood of the century in mid-1993 didn't faze him, although the Coast Guard fine did. The water kept rising and rising with the local rains, and the storms stalled all over the Midwest. Most all of the floodwaters headed instinctively for the tributary ditches that have handled the runoff since the glaciers retreated. They filled up the smaller stems and crept downbound, as ever, with their awful force made more malevolent by the silence. Some of the water backed up patiently behind long, dirt dams that had sat there so long awaiting work that they had become grass-covered parts of the landscape like unusually tidy hills snaking across the rural countryside. But the rains kept falling pretty much everywhere, soaking the rich soils and then flowing off. As they moved along, the flows merged with others, equally full and equally eager to move. And the tributaries began to bulge. When they each reached the main Mississippi, as they were meant to do, it was clear that mankind had a problem.

This 100-year flood on the historic river found that something had changed since the last time. This time there was less room to flow. Since the time of the glaciers, whenever the irregular cycles of excessive moisture had sent an overabundance of water downbound, the flood had fanned out wherever it wanted, over miles and miles of fields and whatever else was in the way, unable to flee and low enough to be covered. And there the water would sit a while, slowly, imperceptibly, and inevitably relinquishing its load of silt to a new setting. That was its job, according to an irregular but immutable cycle of natural reliability. The water might sit there some weeks while gravity did its work on the suspended silt and on the mass of backed-up downbound water.

But this time the backup was worse. It was as if every science teacher, every math teacher, every English and social studies teacher, every French and Spanish and even every home ec teacher in every high school for many miles around had suddenly and simultaneously dismissed every rambunctious teenager into the same small hallway at three P.M. Confined between the pastel-tiled walls, the heads with all the ponytails and reversed baseball caps had nowhere to go; instead of bobbing along normally toward the doorway and the idling buses to freedom outdoors, the flood of teenage humanity would just stack up one against another by all the lockers all along the narrow hall and then back up through every open door into every aisle in every classroom.

Hundreds of engineers work earnestly on controlling the Mississippi River on assignment by the distant dons of Congress who may move like a glacier but still think Nature's antics are subject to solution by appropriation. Such an attitude is understandable given the pressures of television politics to produce clear-cut solutions every day by the six P.M. news and the obvious success of these absentee owners' social engineering efforts in American cities. So, the funds having been properly appropriated after dutiful hearings, mind-numbing reams of testimony, and news coverage that almost gets the point, the engineers over more than six decades set out to fix this river once and for all. After the first couple of dozen years, "controlling" a river that had yet to object to being controlled actually seemed to make some sense.

Entire engineering careers have been spent on this single ribbon of moving water since the early nineteenth century, when Captain Henry Miller Shreve first proposed fixing the waterway by removing miles and centuries of accumulated logjams. That prompted an early, emotional, and precedent-setting constitutional debate over federal involvement in internal improvements among states. There was less concern over the human hubris that fuels such notions of fixing Nature; it seems invisible at the time but slowly appears later, like a Polaroid photo left on a coffee table to develop by itself.

The impetus for this river engineering, of course, was not a charitable concept to help out Nature. Straightening and "maintaining" a river that drains more than one third of the United States by draining the United States Treasury of billions over decades is not a notion proposed by the Salvation Army. Nor is it proposed by a people overly concerned about a river's flow time being wantonly wasted in so many switchbacks.

No, it is typically tied intimately to a shifting consortium of commercial and political interests assembled and long maintained by skilled politicians and lobbyists justifying their own necessity. The voters who regularly pay episodic attention to these doings equally regularly denounce these pork barrel projects, unless they're a beneficiary of pork this time or their house was flooded last time. That's where the consortium-assembly skill comes in, including just enough members and defusing just enough opponents to move the project ahead for now, subject to skilled adjustment anytime, starting tomorrow. And on and on it goes over the years.

Hopefully, given the shortening attention span of very busy Americans in recent times, when the river returns next time to go pretty much wherever it darn well wants to once more, the responsibilities for this expensive failure will be much murkier than the waters that trickled over the first rocks at the outbound end of Lake Itasca, many miles before when the water—and the idea—was clear and pure. After all, who could blame farmers or homeowners or recreational land developers for farming or homeowning or developing in an historic floodplain that hadn't been historically flooded in decades? They had as much right to do their thing as those who came before, didn't they?

These people had paid good money for this land and their banks had loaned valuable mortgage money, and it had all been insured properly and okayed by the elected officials and appointed bodies who would need the landowners' support later. And the local congressional representatives were only responding to clearly demonstrated needs by approving millions of dollars in construction projects to protect these investments with levees and dams. And, in adding their votes to the total, some not so local congressional colleagues were only responding to the same clearly demonstrated needs, trusting in the time-honored power of reciprocity when the hurricane or tornado or earthquake or wildfire struck their district. And when, inevitably, the flood, the rains, the winds, the quake, and the flames do arrive, along with the TV crews to chronicle the colorful chaos "Live," the votes will be there again to make good on the expensive repairs. No one can build levee walls anywhere to withstand that kind of public pressure. The first politician to stand on a wall of sandbags beside a rampaging Mississippi River and tell an assembled throng of homeowners, "Clearly, you should never have built here in the first place," will get the Nobel Prize for courage and, simultaneously, be unelected.

They really are a fascinating natural spectacle—the politics of rivers, that is. Well, both the dynamics of the Mississippi River and its politics are fascinating. They both rise cleanly somewhere with a destination that's fairly clear.

They both start the journey that winds all over, inexplicably unless you understand the invisible internal forces at work. They both pick up considerable cargo along the way, becoming fairly murky to the casual eye. They both have an inexorable power. They both have some predictability—the river water will inevitably flow downhill and the river politics will inevitably flow to the money. And both will change the face of the countryside forever and touch the lives of millions along the way.

Here's how the river and its politics merge: The Mississippi for most of its natural life went pretty well wherever it darned well pleased, according to its volume. The more water that flowed, the more area the river covered, delivering its moisture and, most important, its silt to build up and later rejuvenate the land. Mankind was naturally drawn to the riverbanks for water, of course, but also for the animals that wanted water. Archaeological digs in the Delta found spear points and the remains of the hunted including mammoths, who could be attacked from the banks as they lumbered back from drinking.

But while the animals commuted to the river, humans tended to stay and settle, building homes and establishing farmfields and sizable communities. Nineteenth-century riverboats delivered goods and more people to each stop. By the 1920s, millions lived along the Mississippi. So that when the river overflowed in the great flood of 1927, millions of dollars in property damages occurred, millions of people were displaced—and 214 were killed.

Controlling rivers was not a twentieth-century invention. In 1824, two pieces of unprecedented federal legislation were passed, albeit after another of those long-simmering debates over the role of the federal government. One of the laws was the Survey Act, which directed the Corps of Engineers to survey the Mississippi and Ohio Rivers, both on the brink of becoming frontier transportation interstates. The Corps was a natural place for a young awkward country to turn. Without private or state engineering schools, the nation's cadre of engineers was largely trained by the military at West Point.

The other piece of legislation ordered, among other things, federal clearing of the historic rivers of snags to enable and promote development. Since the river was formed, it had been eating away at its own banks, and trees had been falling into the water. At numerous places they would entangle like colossal beaver dams, sometimes many miles long. Elsewhere, the trees would sink and wait, like wooden torpedoes, for the fragile hull of one of the growing numbers of steamboats about to enter their golden age.

This was clearly unacceptable to any true believer in Manifest Destiny. And so the Corps began unsnarling these knots of wood. Funding was often erratic, given the continued debates over federal powers, which would bubble along and erupt regularly until the military exigencies of the Civil War brushed them aside.

Clearing nature's logjams amid working waterways was a tricky business, involving politics as well as nimble scrambling, sawing up, and pulling out shifting logs to float away, burn, or sell as lumber. Much of this river unraveling was privatized. And one of the entrepreneurs was Captain Shreve, who later gave his name to the Louisiana port. Captain Shreve even invented the snagboat as a safer working platform.

So the idea of "fixing" a bothersome river was not brand-new when, in 1927, the waters rose once more so menacingly. This time, however, there were many more people and structures in its floodplain. That flood was so large, so deadly, and so frightening to so many, even before television, that to this day in some areas it is still capitalized, as in The Flood of 1927 or simply The Flood.

The comprehensive federal flood control legislation that immediately followed this disaster was a logical expansion of Washington's ambitions and a typical congressional overreaction to bad news. The legislation ordered the Corps of Engineers to imprison one of the largest rivers on earth inside a channel, like a convict. Over the ensuing decades the nation has spent billions of dollars to construct on the Mississippi more than three hundred flood control dams and hundreds of miles of levees, dikes, and revetments that help drain one third of the country. So large is this 1927 flood control project that it isn't scheduled for completion before 2010.

It is a vast plumbing project—together with the Interstate Highway System, one of the most colossal construction jobs in human history—designed to make electricity and to steer the river. Besides the implied assurance of ultimately preventing all floods by a misbehaving waterway, part of the package to improve the political palatability of intentionally flooding land behind dams was the promise of a recreation economy with the intoxicating possibility—and sometimes the reality—of Jobs.

Now Nature hates straight lines. It's Western engineers who love them—they make for the more rapid disposal of water and more rapid movement of the cumbersome barges lumbering up and down with the bulk grains and liquids that move so much more cheaply on water. Straight lines make for a shorter river; they also make for less room to store the same volume of rising water en route. Inside thousands of miles of mammoth earthen walls, the water is prevented from spreading out. It can only go up.

The historic flood of 1993, one of those natural phenomena that teaches humility even to engineers, came from one of those unplanned meteorological coincidences that Nature counts on to keep its resources roughly in balance over longer cycles than riverbank dwellers prefer to ponder. After some years of drought, several wet weather systems simultaneously stalled over the headwaters and tributaries of the Mississippi as far upstream as Montana, where the Missouri rises.

All the rivers continued their task of draining the fluid out of the Heartland, but could not drain it as fast as it poured in. Where the water could, it spread out. Where it couldn't, the water piled up—and up and up. Invisibly, it sought the weak points of man-made defenses. The massive weight of the water undermined levees, suddenly bubbling up from below behind the earthen bulwarks and gouging a gap through them, as flood workers fled the crumbling wall. At times like these, it seems so insensitive to ask stunned homeowners what they were thinking when they chose to live in the potential path of a rampaging river. And at other times when the waters have yet to rise, such questions seem so hypothetical.

The Quad Cities of Illinois and Iowa are familiar with the Mississippi and its moods. The river is always there, sometimes visibly moving, sometimes somnolent. It's a part of life. For nearly half of the area's three hundred fifty thousand residents, the Mississippi River is—flood or not—something to cross often. Radio traffic reports focus on the bridges; there aren't that many travel alternatives.

Jim Slavens does not cross the river to work. But as the water rose in the spring and summer of 1993, Jim watched his boats rise—and rise. He watched the waters rise to within six inches of the swimming pool at the house where he raised his children. Everyone saw the water rise. Every inch was carefully chronicled on the radio. One thing that Americans, along with Bosnians and Somalis and anyone else in trouble quickly learns, is that a flood of sorrow or water quickly attracts a flood of television crews with their beltloads of batteries, their fifty-thousand-dollar Japanese cameras, their big-eared satellite trucks, and their inquiring minds.

Now if there is one thing that television crews do not want to see, it is normalcy. Which is why we watch. Normalcy numbs TV minds. Normalcy sells nothing. How long would you stay tuned to Live! news coverage of some suburban strip mall with Hondas, pickups, and delivery trucks coming and going normally? With women, who didn't expect to be on TV, portaging wiggling infants from car to grocery and back a few minutes later without incident? No sirens. No whirling cop lights. No sheet-covered corpses. Where's the news or entertainment in that?

Davenport drew the most TV coverage in the flood of '93 because Davenport had the least flood wall. What's the point of living on the river, Davenport's leaders decided years ago, if you erase the view with a large levee? Other communities were more protective. But Davenport did without walls. So it had to put up with the TV crews cruising the streets that ended in water, crawling all over the sandbags, sticking microphones in the faces of a few dozen stricken property owners. And the images went out to the world watching with curiosity and mild awe during dinner as a great flood was turned into the same kind of edited entertainment as the Persian Gulf War or a sitcom, minus the stars' huge salaries and the canned laughter.

Jim Slavens watched his boats rise by a good twelve feet, which would have given him and his minifleet even more clearance had it not also caused the United States Coast Guard to close the rampaging river, citing safety reasons in the fifteen-mile-an-hour current. That was nearly four times the usual spring pace and fifteen times the normal summer current, when the warm waters obediently drift down toward the next dam. As an incentive to comply with the boating ban, the Coast Guard threatened a twenty-five-thousand-dollar fine for any boaters caught out there, a sum that inspired widespread human obedience. Jim Slavens complied.

The fifty-one day closure of this major thoroughfare caused major confusion and considerable costs for commercial shipping companies, which count on the taxpayers and the Coast Guard to keep this inexpensive river shipping route open and under control. The closure also caused Jim Slavens to get married and go away for a honeymoon. Why not? He couldn't use his boat at home.

This flood was somewhat different in Davenport from the one in 1965, when schools were closed and everyone rushed to help at the flood walls. For one thing, several dozen destroyed homes were not rebuilt in the floodplain. And when the 1993 flood came, schools were already out. Most people watched on TV at home. Only three of Jim Slavens's bank customers were adversely affected by the passing waters, and some of them had been floating into financial trouble anyway.

But after the flood Jim bought a new eighteen-footer. "It's time," he said. And there he is four nights a week and at least one weekend afternoon out there, roaring across the muddy water, radio on so loud he might not hear the telephone beeper on his belt. Good thing passengers can't see that the nonflood river bottom is barely forty-eight inches below. Some people might even see Jim's boat as a possible tax deduction. He can entertain there. And what's more memorable to anyone, especially potential bank customers from foreign countries, than a high-speed race along a very famous waterway? One night Jim even gave the helm to a Chinese official, whose broad smile in the wind was not very communist.

A handsome boat is an excellent vantage point to see, at a distance, the many opportunities in the Quad Cities. The economic restructuring of the nation's heartland in the last quarter of the twentieth century has left many empty manufacturing buildings and even more blanks on the résumés of hardworking farmers and workers, though some who fled have started coming home. In three months one year, the Quad Cities lost twenty-five thousand jobs—Case, International Harvester, Caterpillar, and their suppliers. Which is about twenty-five thousand more lost jobs than any of these sons and daughters ever expected when they followed their fathers into these cavernous temples of industry that had always manufactured products and jobs and, surely, always would, because growth is—was—as certain in the American mind as the arrival of each sports season. The factories and work had always been there, like the river.

But these are midwesterners. Hard times tend to

spawn less moaning and more imagination. This is, after all, the region that invented the steel plow and the airplane, and first split the atom. Fatalism has a hard time taking root in these fertile soils delivered from Canada by the glaciers. Any of those would-be pioneers who peered west out of the shady Appalachian woods last century and found themselves staring across some fifteen hundred of the longest, biggest, and most intimidating miles straight through to the Rockies, any of those folks short on self-confidence likely turned right around and returned to the East Coast to convince themselves that everything that really matters was right there anyway. The ones who strutted out of those woods and made it through a generation or two, and their descendants, just knew that despite any adversity, anything is possible, even—who knows—someday a World Series victory for the Cubs.

So, faced with the need to rebuild quadruple local economies, the Rotary, Kiwanis, and Chamber of Commerce types for the Quad Cities got together in a series of ad hoc committees—networking, they call it in the business schools. If anyone was going to be left with a paycheck to shop in their stores, bank at their banks, eat at their restaurants, get their teeth cleaned and cavities filled, and buy the myriad merchandise of middle-class lifestyles, these communities were going to need a lot of new jobs, even if they no longer paid eighteen dollars an hour with guaranteed overtime. These boosters went recruiting, not with worn copies of Sinclair Lewis's *Babbitt*, but with colorful new brochures extolling everything from export zones and tax abatements to interstate intersections and sewer rates. They formed nonprofit corporations to take the old factory hulks off the new conglomerate's hands for one dollar. They subdivided the aging structures, creating new indoor industrial parks. City authorities wanted these properties back on the tax rolls, so they helped newcomers. So did the utilities and potential suppliers. It was like Rush Week on fraternity row. There may have even been some entertaining on the river, at the club, or in some private homes to expose would-be business owners to the Midwest's small-city lifestyle. Not by coincidence, there were even real estate brokers and bankers on the committees to help arrange financing.

Pretty soon, some new companies sprang up from within and from away. They were smaller enterprises, to be sure, but more innovative, imaginative, eager to seek any market niche. One nearby company even began processing the jillions of grocery store coupons and product rebates that Americans have become addicted to. Everybody used to think you had to make the whole engine to make money. But there are mighty good profits to be had in processing coupons or merely making exhaust flanges, if you make them efficiently. There's even a foreign trade zone and a sense of growth now in the Quad Cities, and hope. At least out in the afternoon sunshine on a shiny boat that's paid for, rocking gently in a muddy river that's well behaved.

Over there, easing away from the dock, charcoal warming on the afterdeck, is the *Jaydee*, the large, floating corporate entertainment platform for John Deere (J. D., get it?), the farm machinery manufacturer that hasn't gotten around to laying off its boat crew yet. There's Tom in his boat; he's a dentist. And Barb. Bernie doesn't seem to be here today.

They work hard, these mid-continent entrepreneurs, to get the nice things that they and their families want. Most days, for instance, Jim Slavens begins the seven-minute commute to his bank by six forty-five A.M. and doesn't leave the office until six P.M. His dining room table at home is given less to elegant crystal and silver than to piles of bank papers and regular evenings of hard work until the ten o'clock news, followed by the five or six hours of sleep he allows himself nightly. Jim's reward is the river, always there in sight or in mind, even if he can't always be on it. "It gets in your blood, this river," he says.

So, come the weekends, Jim and Tom and the others are likely to tie their boats together in mid-river, pass out cold beer and warm burgers, exchange golf scores and gossip, maybe watch part of the Cubs game, and eyeball who passes by and who doesn't. It's the kind of thing people used to do from their front porches before television and air-conditioning drew so many inside or out back onto the deck behind the fence.

On the river, of course, there is also sunbathing, waterskiing, or tubing for the foolhardy or those who know well where the slightly submerged rocks lie in wait. Some people say there's even been some skinny-dipping off Campbell Island at night, although that's only a rumor. There's biking along the eastern shore on that new eight-mile-long bike path; whatever would American bike manufacturers do without abandoned railroad tracks? History buffs have some old Indian battlegrounds to reconstruct. More birds to watch, too, it seems in recent years, even eagles at times. Sometimes Jim or others will take their boats upstream for several hours, go through the locks, have dinner at one of a growing number of riverside restaurants, perhaps ride their bikes a ways, and stay in a bed-and-breakfast overnight. That's particularly popular when the leaves are changing into their autumnal ambers and golds, colors that look pretty so long as they need not be raked.

Naturally, and to many fearing pollution inexplicably, there's also river fishing going on at all seasons. Or at least it looks like fishing from this distance with a line running out of the water to the end of a pole and back down the pole into a battered boat and a reel being held by gnarled old hands belonging to a man who shaved several days ago.

"Hi there! Catch any fish?"

"Who wants to know?"

"Well, uh, I'm writing a book about the Mississippi River and the people who live and work and play along it. My name is Andrew. What's yours?"

"I don't have a name. I'm from this river. I crawled from the mud one day on the bottom of the river. I grew wings and I flew away to become a fisherman on this river."

"I see. So you are fishing. That looks a lot like a fishing pole. Catch anything?"

"That's classified information."

"Do you, by any chance, fish for the Department of Defense?"

"What?"

"Nothing. Do you need any more beer?"

"Nah. I still got some."

"That's surprising."

"What?"

"I said, have a nice day."

Then, it came into sight. It was huge. It was noisy. It was very white. It was the past and the future afloat together. Almost departure time for the *President* riverboat casino, one full football field, several levels deep, of slot machines and tables covered with green felt, greenbacks, and the hopes of suckers from as far away as St. Louis. By the busloads they come, and pay to leave their money on board.

It has become a mantra of modern America that we must have Economic Development. It used to be called growth, back when it was a given. But the changes of the last two decades in the United States have shaken the givens, the foundations of expectations that made life so predictable and so comfortable for so long. Father's income no longer supports a family. Most mothers go to work. So do most women. Most children, including the one third born to single women, will spend some of their youth in a single-parent household. In some cities, a majority of births occur in fatherless families, with all that augurs for the children and society. In fact, most families now do not have children.

Even growth, as a given, has become associated somehow with bad things like crowds, developers, reduced personal space, and possibly pollution that can actually be seen. Better to call it Economic Development. Who could possibly oppose Economic Development? It's like Education or Health Care or any of the growing number of areas that no one can oppose and no one can afford.

The gambling boat *President*, Davenport, Iowa

Nothing within Economic Development has been passed off as more of a panacea than gambling, which despite all the lessons of history, including some notorious nineteenth-century years on this very same river, is supposedly going to solve many, if not all, of society's problems, like a twentieth-century elixir. Gambling, by the way, is now called gaming in public relations deference to those old-fashioned moralists who might oppose gambling as an addictive, wanton waste of time that produces nothing yet costs society and families plenty. Gambling is what gangsters and bookies used to do in sin cities like Las Vegas. Gaming, on the other hand, can be done by families in reconstituted communities such as, well, Las Vegas. And it can be done by respectable, quite possibly even churchgoing people who until now had nowhere to legally indulge the dreams of sudden riches that have lurked in the human heart since even before Midas and Publishers Clearinghouse. But why make families go all the way to the middle of the desert to dream?

In a way, you see, by permitting the rampant growth of gambling, er, gaming, everywhere from Indian reservations to riverboats to convenience-store lottery machines, government and casino owners, who always happen to live far from their casinos, are really helping to promote—are you ready now?—Economic Development. Jobs for people who shuffle cards and break twenty-dollar bills into rolls of quarters. Well, you know the service industry is the coming thing. And who, outside of hypocritical church basement biddies who play bingo every Wednesday night and don't need jobs—thanks to Social Security and their late husbands' pensions—could possibly oppose Economic Development with jobs for families?

Especially if the gaming, er, Economic Development, is packaged as entertainment— what's more innocent than a calliope on a floating adult theme park? And since at times the boat is near the middle of the Mississippi River, that means that, technically, the gambling really isn't happening inside Iowa, sort of. And, hey, nobody holds a gun to the heads of the thousands of Economic Development helpers and makes them walk up the plank past the housewives dressed as dancing girls (except the skirts are longer and the bodices higher) toward the equal opportunity crews of smiling dealers with their string ties, armbands, and shiny vests. Oh, and the Dixieland music—in the humid heart of corn country. And if the shiny vests raise patrons' fears of being taken to the cleaners, those fears may be assuaged by the sight of the ship's friendly, serene, confident and clearly competent, graying captain. (Why are beards reassuring on ship's captains but disgusting on the riders of Harleys?)

In recent years, gambling specifically, and tourism in general, have come to be perceived as the economic saviors of countless communities up and down the Mississippi River and beyond. Americans seem to have more leisure time because survival—everything from cooking to communicating—takes less time than it used to. Americans seem to have more money. Other Americans seem to have the need to get at that money; how else to explain the invention of running shoes containing flashing lights? But unlike clothing, tourism offers unlimited opportunities for mining wallets from sedentary Americans through gambling and touring scenic Lake Itasca and John Hall's olde hotel in

Wabasha, from the nostalgia of Mark Twain's Hannibal to the schlock of Elvis's actual death house and grave and even farther downriver. In between, there is no doubt bungee-jumping. And tourism, unlike the petrochemical facilities that line the lower river, does not seem to pollute the environment—unless you find numerous out-of-state plates and plaid shorts, size XL, visually toxic.

But here they come up the plank of John E. Connelly's *President* riverboat casino, ready to try their luck. Mr. Connelly is a Pittsburgh developer who, among other things, operates riverboats all along the river from Davenport to St. Louis to a new casino in Biloxi, which isn't on the river—but then gambling isn't recreation, either. The eastern company had to make some adjustments in corporate policies in this midwestern community that is so straitlaced and strict that car bumpers touching in a parking lot is cause for dialing 911. The company quickly discovered that no one wanted to work on Christmas Eve, not even for time and a half. Or that Wednesday-Thursday weekends are not so popular with employees whose spouses have real weekends. Or that on New Year's Eve, which ought to be a Major Party Time, the minds of workers and potential patrons turned to family, television, and popcorn, not to some ersatz Dixieland experience on an overheated boat frozen to its dock in a downtown Davenport abandoned for the holidays.

And then there was the Buffet Problem. Buffets are great for eastern casino companies because they seem to be sumptuous while permitting bulk cooking and minimal waitressing. But buffets are not so great for an eastern casino company because the midwestern diners think the eats are unlimited. The company cannot raise the dinner price because nine dollars already seems like a lot to people who eat out only a few times each year and, when they do, they can super-size their meal for only thirty-nine cents extra. So the eastern casino company passed a new buffet rule: One trip per person to the food table. Naturally, the midwesterners complied; they just filled two plates each on the first trip.

That's the price Pittsburgh must pay for forsaking high-rollers.

The *President* is, according to all company literature, the largest riverboat casino du monde. "The only people happier than you to see you win big on 'The Big One' are our dealers—the friendliest on the Mississippi Strip," says the full-color brochure with more smiling faces than usual around the craps table.

With five decks, 27,000 square feet of open gambling space, and fully 1,200 employees by 1991, riverboat gambling became Davenport's largest employer overnight. In the waning years of the twentieth century in America, that much sudden "economic development" can dissipate old-fashioned moral qualms and seem like the greatest thing since sliced bread (which was also invented in the Quad Cities). The *President* is 100 yards long and 87 feet wide (and fully wheelchair accessible). It was built on the hull of the old riverboat steamer *Cincinnati*. It has 700 slot machines and 43 gaming tables. With a full load of quarters and 3,000 diners who have each downed two plates of food, the *President* clears the river bottom by barely thirty inches.

With a cacophony of whistles and loudspeaker departure announcements, the ship eases into the Mississippi several times a day with hundreds of passengers, nearly two million over the years. It's hard to tell whether the boat is moving. In fact, come winter when the water freezes behind the downriver dam, the boat doesn't move. But year-round the "cruises" still depart. There are afternoon economic development cruises, dinner economic development cruises, moonlight economic development cruises, and even special $4.95 breakfast economic development cruises.

The average customer is forty-five to sixty and, like the employees, is probably not from Davenport. Passengers tend to congregate at first in the gold-ceilinged main gambling parlor, where hopes run high. Bells ring. Lights flash. Smoke rises. The passengers are not an openly talkative lot, though. In fact, they are extremely serious. Although gambling is legal, and an increasingly common activity, the passengers act as though it isn't. They eye strangers closely and refuse to talk. They guard "their" machines while awaiting more change. And they smile remarkably little for people relishing a pleasant evening's entertainment.

Initial state dollar limits on bets and wagering were soon discarded, given customers' eagerness to learn about gambling the hard way and the possibilities for profits at the state's ten large casinos. The impacts on gambling addiction were slower to emerge, given the minute news coverage it receives and the absence of excitement in stories like the retired woman who willingly fed her entire savings into the machines' slots.

Very quickly, Pete Mueller fled the noise and smoke to an upper deck. "Win, lose, or draw," he said, "I quit at twenty-five dollars and two beers. That's *my* limit." A retired phone worker who used to fish the river, he and his wife now take a gambling cruise together twice a month. At least they board the cruise together. "She does okay, but she won't let me watch her and she refuses to tell me when she wins." So on this night Pete watched the sunset alone and caught glimpses of a game under the ball park's bright lights while someone's children ran laps around the deck. The Muellers had brought along relatives from Washington state. "He says he doesn't gamble," Pete noted, "but I haven't seen him since we came on board."

In the interests of relieving its customers of the burden of carrying all of their money home, the *President* riverboat casino also has a gift shop offering *President* riverboat casino hats, *President* riverboat casino T-shirts, *President*

riverboat casino sweatshirts, *President* riverboat teddy bears, *President* riverboat postcards, *President* mugs, *President* pennants, even, thank goodness, *President* riverboat casino shoelaces.

In two hours the world's largest riverboat casino is back at dockside and hundreds of economic developers begin, reluctantly, to debark. There is no rush. The neon lights will not go off for some time. And the cleaning crews and the counting crews have all night to prepare the boat for the first morning cruise. At mid-river, meanwhile, a string of sixteen heavily laden grain barges chug downstream with more food for the world. During the long, humid night, without being noticed, they will pass by Buffalo, Muscatine, and the Coast Guard station at Keokuk. They will pass by Fort Madison, where Mr. Schaeffer invented the fountain pen and where the tall, brightly lit stone walls of the nineteenth-century state penitentiary still stand high above the river, forbidding and foreboding. They will pass by the twin bridges of Quincy, and then by a little community that is seeking to turn fictional fame into real opportunity.

You don't know about Hannibal, Missouri, without you have read a book with the name *The Adventures of Huckleberry Finn*. It was written a long time ago about some Hannibal people, including this Huck Finn fellow, by a man named Mr. Mark Twain. He told the truth, mainly. Mr. Twain, that is; Huck is another story. There was things which Mr. Twain stretched, but mainly he told the truth.

But that ain't no matter because that was more than one century ago and far away in a country that had to survive without radios and TV and MTV. And, anyway, whoever heard of a story coming to life outside of Disneyland?

Now, this Hannibal, Missouri, has no business being famous. It looks, smells, and acts like any of scores of river towns that had no real reason for being 'cept for the river. Today, transportation being so different and all, entire minicities can grow up around an airport or even an interstate interchange, although the sense of community is hardly the same within a population that changes planes or even work shifts every eight hours. But older communities like Hannibal evolved by the river and drew their lifeblood from the passing water. Some still do. The river provided food and water and entertainment. And the comings and goings on these reliable waters set the entire rhythm of life for the people on the land.

By chance, anyone could drive from Illinois over the Mark Twain Memorial Bridge, glance to the left at the old downtown, pass by Molly Brown's old house (she of unsinkable fame), and keep driving right on through on Route 36 toward the airport, thinking nothing special about this community tucked so tidily between twin bluffs on the river's muddy west bank.

But by chance, however, a long time ago a special little boy grew up in Hannibal. Like most little boys, he had countless formative experiences and fantasies and sadnesses in his childhood home, neighborhood, and town. Unlike most little boys, however, Samuel Clemens wrote about them. Now, this was not fashionable in the literary life of nineteenth-century America. Since the Revolution, American writers had been largely aping the styles, interests, and cultural conceits of their British ancestors. That was the way things were done back then.

Samuel Clemens was a judge's son. But he didn't know much about—and thought less

of—high society, sitting around a parlor and parlez-vousing. Putting on airs, it was called. So after he worked a spell on riverboats up and down the same river, Mr. Clemens took on his Mark Twain pen name and wrote about real life as he knew it and imagined it on and by the Mississippi River. His characters didn't dress up for dinner. Some of them owned no shoes. They didn't even wash behind their ears, if they could help it. And they talked kind of funny for books, too, using dialect, bad grammar and, dare I say it, slang. Realism, it was called. Not only that, but Huck Finn's story was told entirely from the boy's viewpoint, an almost unheard-of device. Twain's style and realistic details changed American literature forever. And, my, oh, my, how it changed the life of this town over all these generations. Hannibal, the Carthaginian general of Alps and elephant fame, may have thought he made his name famous. Maybe in Carthage. But everywhere else Hannibal is famous as the hometown of Mark Twain, the Abraham Lincoln of American literature, the walrus-moustachioed writer-philosopher whose keen observations and wry musings have taught so many over the years ("Human beings seem to be a poor invention. If they are the noblest works of God, where is the ignoblest?"). Hannibal's literary fame even makes it easier for the town to sell its real-life municipal bonds.

Now, decades after Twain's youth, every year thousands and thousands of pilgrims, many of them from halfway around the world, trek to this little town on the Mississippi River just to see the real place where these imaginings never happened. If you write it, they will come. From Memorial Day through Labor Day, Hannibal's eighteen thousand residents are far outnumbered by the Huck Finn wannabes jamming the motels, campgrounds, restaurants, sidewalks, and tourist sites, most connected somehow to Twain characters or events. From every state and across the oceans, so many come, in fact, spending so many millions of dollars and supporting some 2,500 tourism-related local jobs that some years Hannibal covers half the city budget from its share of the state's sales tax. That's twice as much money as local property taxes produce.

There, in the best commercial tradition of fame, you can find the Huck Finn Shopping Center, the Huck Finn Hoedown, Becky Thatcher's Book Shop, the Mark Twain Outdoor Theatre, Mark Twain's Cave, Mark Twain Country Music Show, the Mark Twain Riverboat, Mark Twain Family Restaurant with its catfish strips, BBQ ribs, and Mississippi Mud Pie, and the Injun Joe Campground featuring Tom and Huck's Go-Karts.

Tom Sawyer and Becky Thatcher are there to greet the visitors in person, parasol and all. You might think, being sophisticated, semirational twentieth-century people, that few folks are going to pay good money for an ersatz literary experience that doesn't even have a hologram or lifelike robot of President Lincoln reciting the Gettysburg Address every twenty-three and a half minutes. But upwards of four hundred thousand people make the literary pilgrimage to Hannibal every year. And the reason has nothing to do with the Mound Builders, who lived around there for centuries, Father Marquette or Louis Jolliet, who passed by, Louis Hennepin, the French monk who stepped ashore there, or the Carthaginian general who lived elsewhere 2,350 years ago but gave his name to the town via a Spanish surveyor. Maybe we can't go home again, if home is our youth. But we sure can try, even if it's the home of someone else whom we remember sharing it with us.

"We're going to see Mark Twain's Cave today!" says Jerry Eyink, who devoured the Twain books in another time and place—more than thirty years ago in his Ohio childhood. Now he and Diane have two little boys. And while Brian and Jeff had yet to read the books, video games proving to be a stronger free-time attraction, they could not help but hear their father rhapsodize often about Tom and Huck and Injun Joe. And they were curious enough to willingly give up a humid summer day at their suburban St. Louis home for the car trip north to Hannibal's humidity and attractions.

All along the back roads their father stops at every scenic lookout to see how different the river looks. Jerry works for Anheuser-Busch in downtown St. Louis just two blocks from the Mississippi. He sees the river out the high-rise's sealed windows several times every workday. And every time, he remembers Tom and Huck, their juvenile mischief with frogs in Aunt Polly's dresser and their lighting out for midnight escapades on the river.

Jerry has always been curious to see Hannibal. Diane is less curious about the town, but does relish her husband's obvious enthusiasm and the rare family togetherness of such brief journeys. And she does remember her parents taking her to the Mississippi's headwaters many years ago. "Are the stones still there to walk across the stream?" she asks.

The popularity of such pilgrimages is part of the touristification of America. Just as, thanks to television, virtually everything has become entertainment, from presidential debates to presidential funerals, from congressional hearings to murder trials and even brief wars. So, too, everywhere—even the world's most obscure nowhere—becomes a tourist destination, if marketed properly. Tourists are a pollution-free industry, their often demanding and rude tastelessness aside. Thanks to American affluence and leisure time, the visitors bring in money, take pictures, and leave town, hopefully minus some of their money. When Hannibal residents think to look out at the Mississippi, they see the river. Tourists look out at the Mississippi and see The River.

Up and down the river, the development of tourism has ignited opposition and enthusiasm, since in many areas traditional American industries from logging to farming have fallen on hard times. Tourism can become both a blessed alternative and a whipping boy for change. Logging is no big deal anymore around Hannibal. Since farming has plummeted as a reliable, survivable occupation, so too have rural land values. The rise of the precisely programmed just-in-time factory delivery system has enabled pipelines and trucks to siphon much cargo from the slower serendipity of river transport. The barge tows don't even stop at Hannibal anymore; they drop off and pick up barges five miles downstream. The only boats that still pause at Hannibal are on the *Delta Queen*-type journeys back in time.

Not too many people are going to travel far to watch the annual swarming of the Hannibal area's willow bugs, even if the bugs' carcasses get so thick in places that a road grader is required to clear the way. So that leaves the town to market Mark Twain, who is dead and can't aim his sardonic style at such goings-on.

"A lot of locals are not so keen on tourism," says Mayor John Yancey. "We don't want to become another Branson, Missouri." The opponents of tourism are typically not in the motel or restaurant business. They probably have not read much Twain and profess pride in that. "I know he wrote some good books," says Claude Lehenbauer, a firefighter and lifelong Hannibalian who hates to fish. "But I never read them." The tourism disparagers dislike the summer crowds, the traffic, the strangers milling about looking different and unaware of local courtesies. "Mark Twain is not coming back," says the mayor, capsulizing the opposition's attitude. "Yet y'all still waiting for him." So pessimistic are some people about previous unfulfilled promises of progress, and so perversely proud are they of Hannibal's backwaterness that many tell the story of the visitor who spotted an immense black storm cloud looming to the west. "Don't worry," he was told, "The Chamber of Commerce would never let anything big come into this town."

But Twain is already here, a fact underlined and sometimes even exaggerated for commercial effect by the Chamber of Commerce, with the more than cooperative help of the local newspaper. And if any of the proposed highway construction projects become reality, Hannibal will find itself a tempting exit on major Chicago–Kansas City and St. Paul–St. Louis routes. "Like it or not, sooner or later," admits the mayor, "Hannibal is gonna boom."

It's not easy living up to fiction. The Hannibal preserved on paper as St. Petersburg was an innocent, vivid, very human place where girls wore ribbons and petticoats, ignored the awkwardness of youthful males, and sometimes awarded priceless smiles to their would-be princes. It was a small-town time when the worst thing a boy could do was tell a lie or smoke a corncob pipe, and scolding aunts, free of the fear of abuse charges, led miscreants away by the ear. It was a graffiti-free time full of superstitions and childhood imaginings, where an old cave might still contain a blood-thirsty crew of river pirates, and where a Mississippi island could be a secret hideout. In those times and that place an unarmed gang of barefoot boys blissfully ignorant of hallu-cinogens could give each other the secret cat signal beneath bedroom windows at midnight; they could light out together to check their fishing lines on Jackson Island and forever fruitlessly plot to rob and ransom people, whatever that meant.

Considerable has changed. No one sober skinny-dips much anymore anywhere. Any food consumed in mid-river generally comes in the form of fried chicken in paper buckets. Grain elevators have replaced the old piers. The shoe factories have come—and gone. A cave visit costs five dollars. Young people, like as not, dream not of life on the river but of moving away after high school graduation. But the noon siren still goes off on time and so does the ten P.M. teenage curfew, although true to Tom and Huck's tradition, no one pays any attention to it. And come spring, the trees still bud out with that beautiful green mist announcing April. The crickets begin their hidden chorus around dusk. And the competitions culminate for this year's Tom and Becky.

It would hardly do for a city that is a mecca of nostalgia as the hometown of Tom Sawyer and Becky Thatcher not to have a real-life Tom and Becky to make personal appearances. And so every year the city's seventh-grade teachers pare the eighty applicants down to twenty would-be Beckys and twenty would-be Toms, who give speeches to the committee of teachers that selects the ten Tom and Becky finalists. But the selection process is no child's play. There are homemade costumes and interviews and walk-throughs. During The Interview, a select committee of Chamber of Commerce types sits in stern judgment in the scariest day of each youngster's short life. The questioners focus on Twain trivia and also seek composure and friendliness in the candidates. They select the year's main Tom and Becky, as well as four pairs of alternates. As befits living caricatures of fictional persons, the Beckys are perfect little ladies just like Becky, but the live Toms are nothing at all like the fictional Tom; they get excellent grades, sit on Student Council, and think that hookey is a mispronunciation of some game on ice.

Announcement of each year's Tom and Becky winners is guaranteed to be Page One news in the *Courier Post* and establishes the precocious young couple as certain celebrities, status they keep even after their reigns end.

Take Nathan Beucke and Libby Minor, both fourteen and both recent winners. Before becoming caricatures together, they had shared only history class and one cafeteria food fight. Now, here they are as living symbols of people who never lived. After a year and hundreds of joint appearances (yes, they are closely chaperoned), they are poised in public and clearly know each other well, handing off memories and conversational gambits without looking, like unusually young old-marrieds.

And do they look perfect for the parts. Whether they're presiding over the grand opening of a new store, reading to kindergartners, visiting sick seniors, greeting the *Delta Queen,* riding in parades as far away as California, or waving to a sellout crowd on Tom and Becky Hannibal Day at a St. Louis Cardinals baseball game, there can be no doubt that these two are the Real Thing. Until you see their alternates an hour later strolling the sidewalks downtown and posing for pictures with scores of giddy parents and embarrassed children.

There's Libby sitting there, her ankles properly crossed and wearing pantalets and a gingham and lace pinafore, which her mom has twice let out in recent months, with a sunbonnet, a parasol, and lacy white gloves. "I don't want to get too frilly here," she confides. "I'm not Little Bo Peep." She carries her school slate and a small purse containing a handkerchief, some dried pansies, a Bible, one peach pit, a good luck buckeye and blue stone, marbles, and chalk. And, since Becky was an independent young woman long before young women were expected to be independent, she also carries her own candle for unexpected cave visits.

And here's Tom—yup, that's him for sure with the mischievous twinkle in his eye—wearing a frayed straw hat, checkered shirt with a stiff collar that was once white, with suspenders holding up faded gray woolen trousers, which are not so cool on Missouri summer days. But the show must go on. He carries, naturally, a genuine willow fishin' pole and a burlap pouch containing necessities for a nineteenth-century youth—a dog collar, a knife handle, a useless key, a tin soldier, a chunk of candle, a blue stone to match Becky's, a glass stopper, one dead pinchbug, a good luck buckeye (in case there are no dead cats around), twelve marbles, a doorknob, a slingshot, a piece of chalk, four pieces of matter said to have once been orange peels, a spool, and several Sunday school tickets attesting to his memorization of Bible verses, tickets Tom acquired in the fence whitewashing trade to cover up his absence from Sunday school. And Tom is, of course, barefoot, which enables him to play with his toes during an interview and explains why he chooses to patrol the shady side of each street for picture-posing.

It was pretty well determined years ago by Libby's mom, a former alternate Becky, that her daughter would vie for Beckydom someday. Nathan's family always assumed his twin brother, Nicholas, had the best shot at Tomdom. But you know how it is with brothers and competition. Nathan's brother may have won the family waterskiing competition on the river because Nathan's swimsuit fell down and tripped him during a final run. But Nathan was determined to win the Tom contest with his outgoing personality, his charm with little children, and his hard-earned knowledge of Twainiana. He heard his first Tom Sawyer story from Mrs. Carmichael in kindergarten but found the old dialect tough going, until he had to study for The Interview.

Libby had seen one of the Huck Finn movies. "It's hard not to be aware of Mark Twain when you live in Hannibal," she says. "Hannibal can seem kind of boring when you're young unless you're into miniature golf or go-karts."

Both Libby and Nathan traveled widely and made many new friends during their reign. They learned some things about real people, too. Old folks reacted the most enthusiastically to their arrival. Americans knew the least about Tom and Becky, but wanted to pose with them the most. Foreigners cared the least about photos but knew the most about Twain and wanted to know more: Where's Twain's house? Becky's house? The whitewashed fence? Which island is Jackson? They want to know where Tom Blankenship, the model for Huck, ended up. (In the California gold fields.) What happened to Samuel Clemens's mother after her husband, the judge, died of pneumonia? (She moved to Iowa with her other son, Orion, the model for Sid Sawyer, Tom's brother.) And, of course, all visitors want to stand down by the water to smell it and feel it moving by so powerfully.

These include Harry and Jean Jones, and Jack and Mike, who are all staying twenty-six miles out of town at a six-dollar-a-night campground for the week. The wife and kids are touring the museums while Harry strolls. Actually, he's just walking. Harry grew up over in Illinois where he skinny-dipped as a boy in the Mississippi River. His father invested thirty-six years of labor in an International Harvester plant that has now been closed and conglomerated. Harry has never read the Twain books and has no plans to do so. "To tell you the truth," says the truck driver glancing around for Jean, "I had a bit of a time getting excited about taking some of my vacation in this place."

He's swum and fished and boated on this river. But walking around on its banks looking in shops and museums would not be his Number One choice for a summer afternoon when the Cubs are playing. "They're talking about bringing in more gambling in Rock Island to bring in more tourists," Harry says. "We need the business. Whether we want gambling is something else."

And the legions of visitors include the Eyinks who saw the cave, the Clemens house, Becky's house that's now a bookstore and strolled—actually strolled—the small town's streets that look so familiar to mid-Americans and so quaint to others. These are the kinds of streets where pedestrians dare to make eye contact with each other and usually exchange greetings involving the weather or upcoming high school game. It was a long day for the Eyinks, more evocative for Jerry than anyone else. But the memory of the river and its famous town is strong enough to still come up for re-sharing at the dinner table now and then.

Few visitors, however, think to wander a few miles west of Hannibal to a tiny rural community with more gravestones than living residents. There, beneath the cedars in the old Big Creek Cemetery lies a quiet, forgotten indication of the continuing impact of Huck and Tom more than a century after they first lived along this river in the imagination of one man.

A granite headstone marks the final resting place of Laura Hawkins, who was a pretty little girl when she lived across the street from and caught the eye of an awkward little boy named Samuel Clemens. Many years later Mr. Clemens confided a secret to his former playmate. It was a secret that she kept throughout her life, but could not keep in death.

And so Laura Hawkins's gravestone, which she dictated, carries two names. One is Laura Hawkins, who died in 1928. The other is Becky Thatcher, who lives on.

The riverboat *Mark Twain,* Hannibal, Missouri

The Hotel Mark Twain, Hannibal, Missouri

Lock and Dam 22, Saverton, Missouri

Lock and Dam 22, Saverton, Missouri

Dean Hood, deckhand aboard *Cooperative Vanguard*,
Lock and Dam 22, Saverton, Missouri

James E. Slavens, President, Northwest Bank & Trust Company, Davenport, Iowa

Gambling below decks on the *President*, Davenport, Iowa

The flood of '93, Davenport, Iowa

The flood of '93, Davenport, Iowa

Awaiting the flood of '93, Moline, Illinois

The flood of '93, Moline, Illinois

The flood of '93, Davenport, Iowa

The flood of '93, Bettendorf, Iowa

Aboard the U.S. Coast Guard Cutter *Sumac*

Retrieving buoys aboard the U.S. Coast Guard Cutter *Sumac*

Aboard the U.S. Coast Guard Cutter *Sumac*

Master Chief Morris, the U.S. Coast Guard Cutter *Sumac*

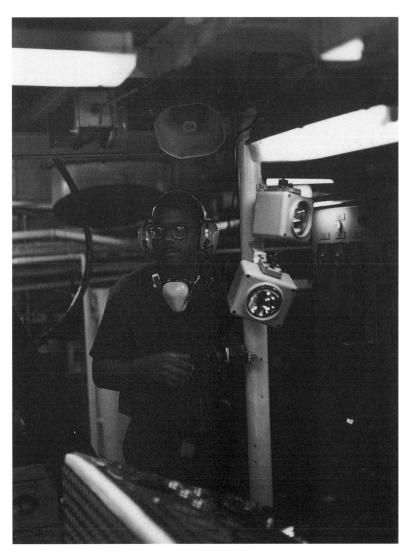

Duane Johnson, Chief Engineer, the U.S. Coast Guard Cutter *Sumac*

Moonlight, Olive Branch, Illinois

The junction of the Ohio and the Mississippi,
Cairo, Illinois

FedEx, Memphis, Tennessee

OUT ON THE WATER

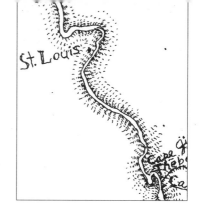

Every several miles along the Upper Mississippi River the traffic tends to congregate in a narrow width of water, a lock that sidesteps a low-lying dam. The river's twenty-seven man-made obstructions are nothing like the towering goliaths of concrete named Hoover or Grand Coulee spanning the vast waters of the West and sending their mighty megawatts hurtling along thick webs of wire toward distant cities that emit a muffled glow beneath their caps of smog.

Mississippi River dams are low and squat, wide, very wide but low, very low. In fact, much of each dam's width is actually a row of heavy doors that can be opened or closed to let nature take its course or back the water up to a depth of nine to fifteen feet, just enough to let the barges clear the bottom's muddy shoals. These dams actually form a lengthy series of long lakes, each lake having locked doors at both ends, creating steps of water up and down the river toward the Gulf of Mexico.

The locks become commercial and tourism focal points, since each string of barges must be partially disassembled to fit into the locks, lowered, shoved out the other side, tied up, and then reassembled to chug off to the next cement neck in the river.

People come to watch this routine and perhaps forget their own routine. Tom McAsey, his wife, Teresa, and their children, Patrick and Shane, drove all the way over from St. Joseph, Missouri, to see this sight. Ernie Irvin cruises the roads near the locks because where there are tourists, there is litter, specifically aluminum cans, which he can sell for a profit. Cows come down to the placid river because covering their lower half in water liberates them from the pesky insects of summer. Others come by car and boat to eat at places like Kinder's Family Restaurant & Lounge On—And Sometimes In—The Mississippi River.

Mike Bray and his son Keith come, too. Mike is divorced, like most people who've gotten married in modern times. He is allowed to see his son every other weekend. Most weekends father and son ride their bikes down to the Mississippi and a new bike path. Mike is a refinery worker and an ex-sailor who finds himself drawn more now to the river than the sea. He takes his son there, too. When males are conversing about potentially intimate things, they like to be doing something else so they can escape into a safer activity in case the conversation gets a little too close. "You can cover a lot of things during a slow bike ride along a massive lazy river," Mike notes.

"It's real fun," Keith adds.

But every day, for thousands of workers, recreationists, and even military men and women up and down the narrow, moving community that is the Mississippi River, tying up to a lock is more work than fun. It is also the only physical contact they will have with life on land. As they glide along past homes and highways, bridges and piers, wildlife and waterlife, these boats and barge strings are their own self-contained communities, complete with kitchens, cultures, characters, and even their own floating influenza infestations. They get television stations that drift out of range every couple of hours and VCRs that play weatherbeaten movies, many of them quite explicit and traded from boat to boat. And the boat's bridge officers can use their radios to exchange weather and river news and coded gossip. With cellular phones they can also call their head offices most times within a few seconds.

But life on the Mississippi River has much more to do with a round-the-clock struggle involving strong arms and backs, somnolent tons of bulk cargoes, oily cables, grinding winches, hot thundering diesels, whirling brass propellers, and thirty days without a day off than it does with anything resembling a cultural life, even the one on *Show Boat*. The nature of river life helps explain the emergence of a mysterious man who was first introduced to the Mississippi through Mark Twain's books.

In recent years, despite his own advancing years, this man would appear many evenings at Lock 27, just above St. Louis, on the Illinois side by Granite City. Sweating deckhands would be laboring mightily on some slippery barge deck, looking like colorized Michelin men in their cumbersome orange life jackets, when from above, somewhere just out of sight behind the edge of the lock's scarred old cement wall, a disembodied voice would fall faintly on their ears. "Would you boys like somethin' to read—books or magazines?"

Looking at each other, the puzzled youths would typically shrug and reply, "Uh, yessir, okay."

Moments later, a yellow plastic bucket would descend at the end of an old clothesline. The bucket would be crammed with outdated magazines and a variety of books, possibly even a classic. Later, in their bunks back by the noisy engines where the heat shimmers even indoors, this current generation of riverboat men would thumb through the pages and stumble upon a little message stamped in black ink on the aging paper: "Compliments of Lonesome Jim, Lock 27, Granite City, Ill. 62040."

Hour after hour, long after dark, this Johnny Appleseed of books would stand by that lock, the busiest on the nation's busy inland water system, sorting his reading material into various piles and likely doing a little reading himself, while awaiting the next barge string. He'd wave to the men in the pilothouse, give away several dozen books and magazines, and then, sometime after midnight, he'd drive away in his battered Toyota so obviously laboring under the weight of a full trunk.

Americans love the mysteries skillfully and mercilessly merchandised by modern media, typically in the form of murder and mayhem. Americans are unaccustomed to, even uncomfortable with, innocent or altruistic mysteries like Lonesome Jim, so free are they of blood, bad guys, and the kind of Technicolor gore that makes great special effects. So for most of a decade, Lonesome Jim became something of a minor legend. "I do it," Lonesome Jim, confided one summer's evening as he surveyed the river in both directions for approaching clients, "because I know how awful it is to have nothing to read."

Lonesome Jim, the Mississippi River's librarian, was

actually James Hearon, a bachelor librarian well past sixty. When he left Lock 27 early those mornings, he returned to his three-room, second-floor apartment over on Madison Street to pursue his own reading. "My goal is to read one hundred fifty books every year," he says. "All kinds of books, though I'm a little behind in Shakespeare."

By day, Jim ran a small library at the old Army Supply Depot. If he had written best-selling murder mysteries or tales of horror, Jim might have earned a good income. But because he was merely an excellent librarian, reading, cataloging, repairing, and above all, recommending books and making others enthusiastic about reading through his charity and words, he received only fifteen thousand dollars a year. Such are the values today along Twain's riverbanks. It was Jim's self-assigned mission to introduce as many people as possible to the joys of reading. "I'm selling books," he says. "Mine just happen to be free."

Mostly he gave away paperbacks and magazines collected around town from people cleaning out cellars and attics, as well as a few hardcover books discarded by the library. And some that he had bought and read.

His father was killed in an automobile accident when the boy was only six. So he grew up on his grandparents' farm in Kentucky, reading his Uncle Charlie's dime westerns and his grandmother's romance magazines. "I read everything I could get my hands on," he recalls, "even Oxydol boxes." Then he would climb up on the woodshed to watch the Kentucky clouds and make up his own stories. "I wanted to be a writer, a really keen writer. I'm not, of course. But I deal with words and what other people write."

Jim served in the Air Force and, after studying library science at Washington and Lee University, taught English in Afghanistan, Washington, and rural Kentucky. When he took over the depot's modest library, overgrown bushes obscured the front door and all the books were crammed into two small rooms down a long hall behind some noisy recreation rooms.

Soon the bushes were gone. He planted a flower bed instead; he thought colorful flowers were more inviting to would-be readers. And he saw a parallel between cultivating plants and minds—both blossom. The library grew to twenty thousand volumes, everything from classics to cookbooks, spread out through larger modern quarters with tables and chairs to lure readers to linger.

On Wednesday mornings at eleven, Jim invited all the neighborhood's day-care children for a story hour. He made up all his stories, just as he had on the farm. Somehow, even though his stories didn't involve homicides, Jim always came up with an exciting ending for the children. "Then I tell them," he says slyly, " 'You know, all the books around here are full of exciting stories just like this one.' And you should see them scramble for the shelves."

But Jim's greatest pleasure came from his river work. The lock crews all recognized him. They waved. Some barge workers even left specific yelled requests for the lock crews to pass on to "that book guy." One night just as Jim was lowering another bucket of books to a barge crew, the towboat captain blasted his ship's horn, switched on the loudspeaker, and swung the boat's powerful searchlight onto Lonesome Jim, standing all alone on the lock wall as if the old man was suddenly center stage. "How y'all doin', Lonesome Jim?"

"What a thrill that was!" Mr. Hearon recalls. "They know me!"

But the river librarian's biggest thrill came soon after that. He lowered some books to a waiting crew. When they got them, they didn't say anything, not thank you, not anything. They just sat down and started reading, really reading, right there on the bow. At that moment Lonesome Jim did not feel so lonesome. He thought, "Now isn't that just about the greatest reward I could ever ask for?"

But, wait, there's more to this river story. It seems that a real-life romance novel was being created back in the stacks of Jim's little library.

There was this woman, Barbara Northcutt. For a while she and Jim worked at the same library. She was much younger than he was—twelve months, to be exact. She moved on to other St. Louis–area federal jobs and then to Leavenworth, Kansas. But they stayed in touch, this man and woman who both love books so much. They'd talk books and exchange books and recommend books and recollect books. They'd make those late-night, cheap rate, long-distance lines veritably hum with shared thoughts. Sometimes they'd even read books to each other, so strong is the power of words.

Fact is, after some years of all this, these lovers of books realized they also loved each other. So in 1994, at a time in life when some people ponder a somewhat slower lifestyle, Barbara and Jim began writing a new chapter in their lives. Actually, it wasn't that simple. Jim, being Lonesome Jim, began to plan and practice his engagement alone, a full year before the big day. He got a pile of books to study, mainly poetry. He picked some favorite poems and then memorized them. He practiced his speech and poetry recital. He envisioned where he would take her for the proposal, where she would sit, where he would sit until the actual moment of proposal and the planned slide down to his right knee, the good one. He even practiced producing the ring box and opening it just the right way to dazzle her with the love contained in the jewelry inside, which, truth be known, he had been secretly saving up to buy for a very long time.

When Labor Day weekend arrived, Jim found himself visiting Kansas—not by chance. He concocted a reason for the two of them to revisit a large book store—again not by chance—where he had so often imagined his romantic plot unfolding. Barbara sat in the wrong chair. There were more people around than he expected. And when he knelt and whipped out the ring box, saying, "Grow old along with me, the best is yet to be," the lid was stuck tight. He was so flustered that the actual proposal came out of his mouth something like, "So, by the way, will you marry me?"

But Barbara knew her lines perfectly. "Yes, James," she said.

Nine months later they got married and now live with each other happily ever after just down the street from the Missouri River. (If this were in a book, you might not believe it!)

Barbara works in another federal library in Leavenworth and Jim, well, he went back to school, hit the books, and at the age of sixty-seven became a licensed real estate agent. But books still play a prominent role in his life. He continues to collect old ones and hand them out at local jails, which are not unlike rivers, in the way a steady stream of disparate people forever flow through, sometimes in trickles, sometimes in a flood.

Even in his real estate work, Jim gives away books. He hands out new children's books to every house hunting family in the hope that they will read to each other and, perhaps—not by chance—remember him. There, taped inside the back cover of each book with his smiling photo beaming out, is a business card for James Hearon, Real Estate Agent.

The card says nothing about Jim being lonesome anymore.

*   *   *

Downstream from old Lock 27, just before dawn, another workday begins for CGB 36 and the twenty-two men and women on board. The *Sumac* is a Coast Guard workboat resembling an oversized and overtall tugboat tautly connected by cables to an even-larger 136-foot-long work barge. Built in 1943 and twice rebuilt since, the *Sumac* itself is 115 feet long, a floating wad of engines, generators, and instruments, with living quarters for two dozen humans squeezed into crannies below deck.

The *Sumac*'s job: patrol more than two hundred miles of this major river and oversee commercial navigation. In practice, this means constantly charting the river's ever-shifting bottom and water level and adjusting all navigational aids accordingly, especially hundreds of color-coded metal buoys that must be constantly maintained and moved to mark the safest channel through the shifting waters.

Much about life on the river is little noticed by its neighbors. Ask most residents of Cincinnati, St. Paul, Omaha, Kansas City, Memphis, New Orleans, or St. Louis why their city is where it is and chances are, they think it just erupted there. But for those who live and work on the river, the navigational vigilance of the Coast Guard and Army Corps of Engineers is essential and nonstop, day and night, in fair weather and foul, in winds and sun, in blizzards and fog.

For a downbound string of barges with thousands of tons of grains or petroleum products in an eight-mile-an-hour current, a buoy's being out of place by one hundred feet can mean the difference between safe clearance and a commercial and environmental disaster. A broad-beamed, blunt-nosed, engineless barge is not the easiest thing to maneuver at any time. Tie sixteen of them together, add several thousand cubic feet of moving water, scores of tons of grain, gravel, and petroleum products, some fog, a sharp turn and it's more like trying to herd a couple dozen barrels down a rocky mountainside.

Presiding over the *Sumac* like the master sergeant he would be in the army is Chief Bosun Mate Bert Morris, a Coast Guard veteran who sports a crewcut and the sunken eyes of someone in charge of twenty-two human lives and several million dollars worth of government equipment that stretches one twentieth of a mile long.

Chief Morris (no one dares to call him Bert, possibly not even his wife Catherine) grew up north of Coos Bay, Oregon, the son of a cattle rancher and timber faller, two professions that like boating are subject to the powers of nature. Going to sea seemed natural to the future Chief. So he did, serving nearly two decades in the Coast Guard on all three U.S. coasts, American Samoa, and in Alaska's Inner Passage on a seabuoy tender that was seventy-one feet shorter than the *Sumac*.

Ocean sailors tend to deride river sailors, thinking their own watery domain is larger, deeper, and more dangerous than one with a tree-lined shore just over there. But ocean sailors wouldn't know what to do in flowing water with a mind of its own, water that can double in depth within hours, in a channel that changes overnight, where turns are measured in feet not miles, amid quarter-mile-long barge trains passing so close you can see the towboat captain's cheek bulging with chewing tobacco.

What Chief Morris knew about the Midwest as a youth you could contain in a noon hour grain report. Suddenly, here he was assigned to sail on the Mississippi, almost always within sight of land except during thunderstorms. "The Mississippi River is like life itself," he says squinting into the decaying darkness of a summer morning. "From the distant shore it can seem downright pretty. But up close, it can get a little messy. Anything you can find anywhere, you can find floating down this river—cattle, deer, refrigerators, whole trees, cars, even parts of houses at times."

Up close, the Mississippi looks different. No deep blue, crystal clear waters here. The river is carrying tons of silt per mile downbound to rebuild a Mississippi Delta constantly being eroded by Gulf currents. Some of this silt and the pebbles rolling along the bottom are parts of the Rockies from decades, even centuries, ago.

Another difference between river and ocean sailing is the existence of place names. The ocean may have coordinates. But all along the river on virtually every bend, every island, every physical landmark there is a name. Most of them go unnoted on common maps and remain unknown even to people who live near them on land. They likely have some historical connection, now lost like great-grandparents amid the faulty memories of so many passing years and modern generations of youths preoccupied with now, not yesterday. There's Daniel's Light, Dogtooth Bend, Antelope, Grand Tower, Fountain Bluff, Backbone Bend, Price Daniels, and Uncle Joe Light. These are the names that would still mean something to Mark Twain, who memorized these same waters as a cub, or apprentice, and a pilot until 1860 when the Civil War shut down civilian river traffic. "It was plain," he wrote in "Perplexing Lessons," a chapter in *Life on the Mississippi,* "that I had got to learn the shape of the river in all the different ways that could be thought of—upside down, wrong end first, inside out, fore-and-aft, and 'thort-ships'—and then know what to do on gray nights when it hadn't any shape at all."

Then there is Buffalo Island, which isn't on road maps, doesn't have any buffalo, and isn't really an island anymore, but will be where the *Sumac* will tie up on this night after another long day.

One advantage to Coast Guard river work, at least for married crew members, is the opportunity to get home every week or ten days. Most *Sumac* crew members live in or near St. Louis, where the ship does general harbor work every other week. Other times the boat ranges up and down the river up to several hundred miles as water levels, the availability of other craft, and emergencies dictate. One day the *Sumac* leaves St. Louis at seven A.M. It ties up fourteen hours and one hundred fifty downriver miles later at the levee by Cape Girardeau near one of the gaps in the fortresslike walls that many river cities have erected to protect themselves from the occasional moods of their watery neighbor. On this night two couples, arms wrapped around each other, sit on the weathered stones, oblivious to the boat's noisy engines, staring out at the passing blackness, seeing nothing but each other.

While towboat after towboat passes by on its relentless river errands, the *Sumac* will sit there for eight hours. No need to go ashore. It's the first night of eight away from home on this journey. And Sandy Padgett, the cook and one of four female crew members, has her larders full with, among other things, forty pounds of hamburger, twelve loaves of bread, thirty dozen eggs. She knows Chief Morris likes seafood; so one dinner will be fish. She knows too that Steven Adams, the second in command, likes chicken and dumplings; so it's safe to assume they will appear one evening. Sadly, one lunch will be scallops and catfish, which Chief Adams detests despite his maritime profession. "I'd rather get hit in the nose than eat seafood," he will announce before skipping that meal. On one night, the night Sandy has the most paperwork to do, there will be simple steak and potatoes. Breakfast on Tuesday and

Thursday will be omelettes. And, always, there will be sandwiches available. "These guys would eat sandwiches for every single meal if I let 'em," Sandy says in mock despair.

Like most crew members not assigned to the bridge, once under way Sandy becomes so busy she'll be totally unaware of where the boat is. But when four A.M. arrives, she starts to stir. One by one, so do other crew members, pulling on their light blue work uniforms. The engines are started, warmed, and checked. Same with the instruments, especially the depth finder, which reveals that the river is thirty feet deep at Cape Girardeau, twelve feet deeper than just two weeks before. Sometimes it can rise eight feet in one day. "You get a heavy rain in Keokuk," says Chief Adams, "and three days later we see it go by down here."

Twelve feet more water, one mile across, is a lot of water moving along. It looks pretty from shore. From the *Sumac*'s tidy bridge it means more hassle. It means the *Sumac*'s awakening crew will be moving many more of the five hundred buoys along the one hundred eighty-five river miles between St. Louis and Cairo at the bottom tip of Illinois where the Ohio and Mississippi meet and begin to merge. It's as if highway crews had to move the curbs and center lines of a highway system out and back every few days to mark the new traffic lanes without stopping the traffic. Sometimes, if it's been raining upriver on both the Mississippi and the Ohio, the rivers will be crowding into the same channel. They'll both start backing up before they meet, deepening their channels by several feet thirty or forty miles above the massive junction. The sheer weight and force of this flowing water has likely ripped away several of the 450-pound markers, sometimes up to one hundred fifty of them. So the *Sumac*'s smaller motorboat will be dispatched to scout the overgrown shorelines for strays, towing them back to the ship for refurbishment and future use. Each one rescued saves taxpayers a few hundred dollars.

It is now five-forty-seven A.M. The sun is rising over Illinois, giving shape first to the river banks and then the river itself. An immense tree drifts by, roots and all, another victim of the perpetual bank erosion process. Along comes the *Bethany Dawn* downbound with eight bargeloads of huge rocks for some underwater construction below. "Morning, Cap'n," the radio crackles.

"Morning, Cap'n," Chief Adams replies. It is unlikely that the *Bethany Dawn*'s skipper can see Chief Adams. But it is nonetheless bad manners not to wave to passing neighbors in the elongated neighborhood of this river community. And river protocol requires the waves match each other in style and enthusiasm. "If another captain gives you a big two-arm wave," the Chief warns, "you better get up off your chair right quick and give him back the same." No one wants a reputation for unfriendliness on the river where you might someday need each other. So on this morning each man waves out the window at his unseen friend passing in the darkness. Indeed, neither man has ever seen the other's face.

"Can you imagine driving somewhere on shore waving at every passing car?" the Chief asks. "They'd lock you up pretty quick. That's 'cause there's a different spirit out here on the river."

"Looks like she's up a couple feet," he says into the radio.

"Looks like it," comes the reply.

At five-fifty-seven the United States flag is raised astern. "Cast off!" The hawsers are lifted off the dock. The last crewman scurries up the plank and back on board.

"Spuds up!" The *Sumac* has four long, metal legs, called spuds, to drive hydraulically into the riverbottom and hold the boat in place. These vertical metal beams come up, dripping and muddy. And the *Sumac* eases out into the current for a three-hour businesslike ride downstream to Cairo. Barring emergencies, the *Sumac* performs its work while moving upstream, using a delicate balance of engine power opposing the current's power to hold it in place when necessary.

Downbound, the towboats tend to drift more with the current, using the engines for steering and saving their fuel for the awesome, full-power struggle back upstream. The *Sumac*, however, moves downstream around eighteen miles an hour; Chief Morris knows a full day of full power lies ahead.

The boat passes by mile after mile of undeveloped rural riverbank. Flocks of birds dive for breakfasts of bugs now retreating from daylight. Startled deer scurry up the bank. Some resident ducks paddle in the shallows with their young ones tagging along. Come fall, when their northern cousins follow the river on their genetically programmed migration route south, these creatures had best be somewhere else. Flying fowl attracted to the river in autumn also attract thousands of camouflage-clad hunters in rubber boots who sit in the rented blinds of their hunt clubs along the banks and blast away into the sky, calling it sport.

The boat passes by Thebes, a little river town that was once much larger. "Oh, we had near to one thousand folks one time," says the town clerk, Thelma Foutch. That'd be back after Dred Scott stayed in jail there and Abe Lincoln held court there once or twice. "Right now, Thebes is more like four hundred sixty." That's not counting her husband Samuel and son Dwight, who've both worked on the river, thirty days on and thirty days off for years. They'd run fuel oil from Texas to Wisconsin and pass right by her house on a string of oil barges some nights, and with neither one knowing it.

"The river's got a real personality," Thelma adds. "It don't frighten me exactly, as long as you keep your eye on it." But then, unlike some, she learned her lesson from the regular floods that have convinced whole towns to move away from the riverbank; Thelma lives up on the hill now. She looks out her office window and sees the *Sumac* charge by briskly, downbound.

Below the *Sumac*'s decks Duane Johnson presides over both engines and eight crewmen in a noisy, cramped engine room where every spoken word spoken is shouted. I SAID, EVERY SPOKEN WORD IS SHOUTED. On cool days the temperature in that room sometimes dips to one hundred ten degrees.

Fifteen years ago, in high school, Duane saw some Coast Guard literature and fell in love. He went to machinists' school for free, has been to Antarctica, on Great Lakes fishery patrols, boat inspections, search and rescue, and drug patrols out of Boston.

Though he's belowdecks most of the time, Chief Johnson prefers the Lower Mississippi's openness and vitality over the river's lakelike personality above the locks. In his charge are two 750-horsepower, eight-cylinder D3-79 Caterpillar diesels and three generators putting out a combined 220 kilowatts of power. The *Sumac* can consume upwards of 1,200 gallons of fuel per day powering all that machinery and its three fifty-two-inch screws.

Circling around this massive machinery and its controlled explosions are seven men and one woman, an electrician. Women have served on Coast Guard boats since 1991 with few problems, according to all sides, except that the male sailors seem to swear less. Though enlisted, the *Sumac*'s four female crew members live apart in air-conditioned officers' quarters. But they pull physical duty like everyone else.

"I've had a lot wimpier guys than some of these women," says Joe Millard, the bosun's mate who oversees the tricky and dangerous deck work. "Women don't whine. And if they need help, they ask for it. Take Shelly, there. She's about the hardest worker I've ever had."

Shelly Bennett is a Montana girl, a trucker's daughter, who grew up steeped in the country work ethic along Montana's Yellowstone River, one of the Missouri's tributaries and the last major American river still unfettered by a dam. She enlisted to see some of the world, but did not count on the downriver world outside Montana being so humid—or crowded. The St. Louis metropolitan area alone, where summertime humidity often exceeds the temperature, houses far more people than all the one hundred forty-eight thousand square miles of Montana, where humidity sometimes soars to 25 percent.

Then there's Anne Strachan, a twenty-five-year-old deckhand from upstate New York who's saving her earnings and entitlements to attend college. "I just like being on boats," she says, though she prefers ocean craft. "Boat crews are like families. Everybody looks out for each other. The guys—oh, they're just fine once they see we work hard, too. And they're very protective on shore. They won't let us go into parts of some towns."

By the time breakfast is done, lunch preparation has started and the barge deck is set for work. The *Sumac* reaches the bridges at Cairo, the bottom of Illinois, Abraham Lincoln's home state that stretches farther south than Richmond and a good chunk of Kentucky. The bottom of Illinois is where the Mississippi River and the accents begin flattening out to fit the broader lower river valley profile. In glacial days gone by the Mississippi here, freed from its work of gouging the narrower gorges of the Midwest, would flow in a braided necklace of rivers wandering back and forth over one hundred miles or more of bottom land, irrigating and fertilizing for future cotton and other crops.

The bottom of Illinois is also the end of the North, the place where the Civil War becomes known as the War Between the States. There, one mile below town, at the very rocky end of the state, is a point that early French explorers spotted as an excellent location for an outpost. There, ten days after Fort Sumter, in a tribute to the surviving strategic import of rivers, Union troops established Fort Defiance, what would become one of U. S. Grant's major supply depots and is today a local park that draws all kinds of people from neckers to beggars.

This area is full of history—Louis Jolliet, Jacques Marquette, and George Rogers Clark, who captured the area for colonization by Virginia back when states could do that. Cairo itself was to become an occasional boom town, a community of false fronts, false hopes, and lucrative speculations for waves of shady dealers and settlers over the decades.

The steamboats—sometimes ten or twelve per day—brought in all types of people, savory and otherwise. Their arrivals in isolated communities were full of excitement, promise, and even mystery. The first steamboat passed by Cairo in 1817 en route to St. Louis. The boats, eventually built three hundred feet long and forty feet wide, became specialized for the Mississippi. It was said the boats could navigate on a heavy dew. Actually, medium-sized boats needed only four feet of water, half what laden barges require now. But seasonal variations in water levels often made riverboat travel unpredictable, as did the snags hidden beneath the water and the fires, collisions, and unexpected boiler explosions. An 1867 investigation found at least 133 hulks sunk in the Mississippi between Cairo and St. Louis, almost one per mile. The war stunned riverboat traffic, and the emergence of the reliable railroads, built on an east-west axis through Chicago, was the coup de grace.

Cairo (pronounced KAY-roe) today is a rundown backwater community of crumbling streets, abandoned stores, and stubborn racial divisions that have defied years of well-meaning work. On a Saturday afternoon most stores are closed, except, of course, for the liquor outlet. Windows are broken. Signs are fading, even the one at Dottie's: IF IT'S NEW, DOTTIE HAS IT! But Dottie's itself has had it; the store is long since shuttered.

Fort Defiance, however, is a beautiful setting with views of two rivers, three states, and the three peaked bridges that link them with cars and trucks laden with everything from tourists to watermelons humming high up on these trans-river spans.

Stepping from their car and stretching in the summer heat are Earl and Helen Picard and their grown daughter Arlene, making a twice-yearly pilgrimage to this point to walk down on the smooth melon-sized stones and hear the rushing water on both sides. "I'm not sure why we do it, actually," says Earl. "We did it one time years ago and it just seemed like such a special place." They'll be back again New Year's Eve.

From a bench not far away George Matthews is watching. He is forty-three years old now, the son of a riverboat worker. For forty years George's father worked on the barges. George has worked at times in his life too, starting on a Kentucky strawberry farm at the age of thirteen, though nothing as sustained or hard as riverboat work. In fact, in recent years George hasn't gotten around to working much. He says his back gives him trouble. And the public assistance keeps on coming anyway. So pretty much every day George drives down to Fort Defiance Park to watch the boats and do a modest amount of half-hearted, tax-free begging from tourists like the Picards. This being the 1990s, George starts out asking for ten dollars. He'll really settle for five dollars, however. It's for gas, he says.

The confluence is a truly impressive scene when viewed in person and not confined by a TV screen, as so much vicarious tourism is these days. There is water everywhere, moving massively, inexorably, on its silent mission south.

The water from Pennsylvania, Ohio, Kentucky, and West Virginia arrives from the northeast to join the waters arriving from the northwest from Montana, the Dakotas, Minnesota, Missouri, and Nebraska.

The Mississippi has grown quite large by this point. At Hannibal, the flow averages 73,000 cubic feet per second. That's more than 540,000 gallons of water in one place for one second and immediately replaced by another half million gallons, second after second, minute after minute, around the clock throughout the year. When the Missouri joins the Mississippi just above St. Louis, it adds another 82,000 cubic feet per second, so that when it passes St. Louis, the mighty river is moving by at 190,000 cubic feet per second. At Cairo, the Ohio adds another 278,000. That's about 3.6 million gallons of water, weighing some 30 million pounds, flowing by one point every single second.

At flood times the volume can be six times as large.

There go two of North America's largest rivers, the watery sum total of one hundred thousand lakes, rivers, and streams from thirty-one states meeting and flowing side by side separately for perhaps five miles. Then, slowly, as if finally getting to know each other, the two dirty rivers mingle and merge to move on toward the sea, more than twice as big and even browner than they were apart.

This is a busy commercial confluence. More cargo moves through these arteries here most years on barges than passes through the more famous Panama Canal on ships. Out in the middle of this swirling water, looking much smaller than it was at dockside, is the *Sumac*, slowly swinging around to head back upstream.

To everyone in general and no one in particular, Chief Morris announces on the maritime radio, Channel 13, his turn, his position, and his intentions. Downbound traffic has the right-of-way on the river, especially if it's flying that red warning flag: Explosives.

But river protocol and Chief Morris both dislike surprises out on these treacherous

The flood of '93, Moline, Illinois

waters that hide so many dangers so well. Hence, the frequent announcements amid all these northbound strings of barely controlled barges struggling against the currents to turn right and left, as their rust-red or pastel-colored southbound colleagues fall down to the sea with the agricultural bounty of America's Heartland.

Now, the *Sumac*'s real work begins, monitoring the river's depth, maneuvering the boat and barge, rearranging the buoys, keeping the crew safe, and staying out of the way of downbound traffic. Chief Morris leans into the ship's microphone: "Prepare to pull one starboard." Using his three props, three rudders, and the opposing current, he maneuvers the barge and ship toward a misplaced buoy in mid-river. It's an unusually shaded green. These green buoys come from St. Louis, meaning this one is about two hundred miles from home for reasons never known. Probably it got caught on a downbound string of barges and was dragged all this way. The Chief has encountered other mysteries: buoys from other rivers, some even from up near Chicago.

Joe Millard leans over the edge, hooks the stray on a cable, and it's lifted up, dripping river weeds and refuse and stored for use later back in St. Louis.

There is an impressive industrial choreography to this work. It involves nature and machinery, codes and spoken shorthand, nods, radio commands, and small but significant waves of a hand. And it is all spiced with very real danger and a kind of mechanical, metallic beauty. Engine crews, hidden below decks, tend to their twin diesels, matching their revolutions to the shifting signals from the bridge. There, either Chief Morris or Adams steers and watches the depth gauge, the currents, downbound traffic, and misplaced buoys, positioning a vessel nearly one football field in length so that one life-jacketed deckhand, his belt firmly grasped by another, can reach out to grapple a bobbing buoy and hook it to the crane's cable for removal. Meanwhile, six or eight other deckies repair and prepare other buoys for placement on a wet metal deck littered with chains, buoys, 1500-pound cement blocks and river weeds, plastic bags, and other downbound detritus that come up on buoy chains. It is an understandable irony of riverboat life that the busy crews see so little of the river they work on, so consumed are they by the details of working—and surviving—on the deck in the river.

The loudspeaker crackles a ten-word message that is both plan and warning: "Prepare to set one port and pull one diver starboard."

The new buoy, listing awkwardly out of its watery element, is carefully positioned near the shiny deck's slippery edge. One hundred feet of heavy steel chain with links over two inches long is attached and coiled nearby. The other end is linked to an imposing block of cement, the size of a pharaoh's coffee table.

Chief Adams is on the bridge. No lunch for him today; it's catfish. He's watching the changing depth finder and the shifting engine gauges, which Chief Johnson is also watching intently below deck.

When Chief Adams has the *Sumac* in position, he gives the command over the loudspeaker: "Set one port!" The deck crew steps back, way back from the about-to-be-whirling chain. "Stand clear!" With an impressive *ker-thumk* heard even over the growling diesels, three quarters of a ton of cement is dropped over the side to plummet down into the unseen mud below. With a power and speed that creates a respectful distance even for deckhand newcomers, the chain is ripped off the deck like lightning, link by link, and then the 400-pound buoy flies overboard like a piece of paper. It gets a quick christening beneath the waves and then bobs back up ready for guard duty, rain or shine, as the *Sumac* moves on to the next marker.

The average buoy, which is shaped with metal vanes and painted for maximum visibility even by radar, lasts one year, though many endure a decade or more. Riverbank marksmen aside, the biggest threat to buoys are the beneficiaries of their guidance, the awkward barge tows themselves that come, well, barging downstream and run them over. One captain likened maneuvering a string of barges downriver to moving a blunt pencil through a crooked metal tube without either end touching. This requires precise aim going in and then considerable to-ing and fro-ing, back and forth against the current and then with it, and then back again through another bend where the depth and position of sandbars may have changed overnight.

Many times the overrun buoys bob right back up behind, scraped and bent. Sometimes they are completely chewed up by the towboat's eight-foot propellers or torn loose or dragged out of place. The *Sumac* has a few stashes of buoys and cement sinkers along the riverbank.

Most days, the *Sumac* dispatches a motorboat with chain saws, weed whackers, and machetes. Those crews clear the view of navigational markers and lights on shore while cruising the banks for stray buoys. Every few hours the motorboat reappears with two or three reluctant buoys in tow, like a trio of Tom Sawyers caught playing hookey.

River tradition—"red right return from sea"— dictates that the red buoys mark the channel's right side upbound while green buoys mark the channel's left side. Just ahead is a green buoy nearly in midchannel on the wrong side of the river. It's a "diver," one that likely has lost the underwater fins that help keep it upright. Every few seconds the current pulls the buoy underwater straining against its chain, only to let it bob back up in a slightly different place.

Divers are a menace, sitting there as they do just waiting to cripple a towboat's propellers and let the entire tow of barges crash into a bridge. Chief Adams must move the diver.

But a quarter-mile-long string of barges has just appeared around the bend. There's not much time. Chief Adams applies full power and aims straight for the misleading buoy. If the deck crew can snag it quickly with a long pole, the *Sumac* can drag it out of the way in time. But the bobbing buoy keeps dodging the pole successfully. And the barge string is getting closer and closer, although huge engines sound distant still. What is audible is the powerful rushing sound of water, an awful lot of water, being pushed ahead of an awful lot of steel across the broad, blunt noses of the heavily laden barges now being aimed more than steered. The rushing sound continues to grow louder, like an immense never-ending, always-breaking wave.

Chief Adams makes a quick decision. He backs the *Sumac* out of the main channel. Seconds later, the barges run right over the green buoy, sending it scraping unseen and unheard along the bottom of each passing barge and then beneath the throbbing towboat.

"Sorry, Cap'n," the chief radioes the towboat. "I was trying to get this 'un outta your way."

"Don't you nevermind," comes the reply. "Ah knew zactly whatchew was adoin."

Both men step outside to wave.

There is no written rule that every riverboat captain be born in Louisiana, just as there is no rule requiring all aircraft pilots be born in Oklahoma. However, just as every jet pilot affects the studied stoicism of a Chuck Yeager radioing that a wing has fallen off at Mach 1—"Ah have an anomaly heah"—every riverboat captain must talk Louisiana on the river, even when cruising deep within the bowels of Pennsylvania. River Louisiana is a humid language that sounds roughly like ultra-Southern colored by too much thick coffee and spoken right friendly-like with a mouthful of marbles, or tobacco, or both, and then spiced with static.

To those uninitiated in Mississippi River culture, it seems a wonder that such languid, mush-mouthed communications do not cause every boat to run into every other boat. The language of Louisiana, however, may explain—or, rather, 'splain—the maritime reliance on whistles and colored lights.

With the barge string gone and its wake subsiding in the thick chocolate-looking water, the Sumac moves back to mid-river to retrieve the diver. This time, the wild buoy is successfully snagged. And the crane strains to lift the one-ton load. "Heavy strain forward," comes the report from the deck. The *Sumac* and crane pull harder. Then, as so often happens when the cement sinkers become embedded deep within the ten feet of muck that coats the Mississippi's bottom, the steel chain snaps. "Parted!" comes the report, which is unnecessary because the chief felt the break and the boat's minor surge through his feet. One more chunk of cement is lost below. (What do you suppose archaeologists will discern about our civilization's religious practices when they come upon such cement litter three hundred years from now?) But the buoy is recovered, infested by a crawling colony of annoyed river maggots, quarter-inch worms that settle on many buoys by the thousands for reasons no one on deck thinks or cares about. They are scraped into the river to become something's dinner. After some rewelding and repainting, the buoy is put back to bob about again elsewhere that same day.

"A big part of our job," says Chief Adams, heading back upriver, "is to make sure our kids live through their mistakes out here." Indeed, the entirely enlisted Coast Guard crew does often seem more like a family than a hierarchical military outfit. Crew members do see more of each other than their onshore families. Boat life has grumpy characters and jolly characters, quiet members and gregarious ones. It has running jokes and teasings, familiar tastes and team loyalties, even some passing feuds, as well as a team household routine, even the onerous fire and man overboard drills, that can be comforting in their predictability.

"I can't get enough of this work," Chief Adams adds. "Sometimes out here it's hard to imagine there are other people in the world, especially in the white winters when the banks are all bleak and blue. I like everything about it—the river, the countryside, the scenery, the crew family, the work, the challenges, even the food. And once you push open the throttles on one of these boats and feel the power respond through your feet, you are hooked."

All the while that either chief is on the bridge, he is constantly watching out the windows in all directions, checking the depth finder ("Look, right there's an old sandbar just waiting to make some low-water trouble"), and listening to at least three radios—13 is the maritime channel to talk with other craft and eavesdrop on all river activities, 16 is for emergencies, and 21 is the Coast Guard's working channel. In addition, there are radiophones and cellular phones at hand for instant communication with St. Louis or anywhere, really.

Hour after hour, bend after bend, buoy after buoy, the *Sumac* continues up the river right on through dinner, which is eaten on the run—steak and potatoes on this night because they're simplest and Sandy Padgett has all that paperwork to catch up on. Dusk is approaching. "We work from when it gets light until it isn't anymore," explains Chief Morris. The small boat is recalled from its scouting mission, lifted from the water, and refueled for tomorrow.

Buffalo Island is just around the bend. It is a seemingly empty stretch of riverbank, devoid of people and buildings. The fifteen-foot banks are thickly covered with trees and bushes that hide another stash of buoys and sinkers. The *Sumac* radios its location to St. Louis and noses into the bank. Crew members scramble onshore to tie up the boat, clambering over some very large, very dead tree trunks strewn about by the last flood. For good measure, Chief Morris drives the *Sumac*'s spuds into the river mud like nails. The deck is cleared and cleaned for the morning. Just outside the bridge, a lost ladybug that had landed at lunchtime in mid-river suddenly leaps ashore too. "Finish all engines," Chief Morris orders.

Some crew members will watch a movie on the VCR. One or two will try their luck fishing. Others will lug their bicycles up the bank and find a dirt road to ride for an hour or two in the summer's lazy dusk. Several crew members will fall asleep early. Chief Adams will tune his personal radio to a public radio station, hopefully classical music, and work on the correspondence school courses for his second career after Coast Guard retirement in a decade or so. Chief Morris probably will check in with his wife by phone and certainly will watch his favorite TV show, *Home Improvement,* in his air-conditioned cabin.

Twenty-eight-point-four more miles of river have been checked and maintained one more time on this day. In seven days the crew will be back home in St. Louis. In seven hours the routine will commence again.

For a place so full of life and so constantly changing, the river is surprisingly quiet as night falls, even in summer when it is teeming with life. While the *Sumac*'s crew sleeps soundly, bugs by the billions buzz about. Swallows screech and swoop, beaks agape, to gobble them up. Bats, too, find excellent insect hunting. Fireflies, sure signs of standing water somewhere close by, drift around.

As that thin band of pastel pink light melts away on the western horizon, to begin reappearing on schedule in the east in six hours or so, an amazing blanket of stars quietly emerges above. With the absence of competing city lights, more stars twinkle there than seem countable in a lifetime. These are the same stars that shone down one hundred thousand years ago on the glaciers. Now and then, a star falls, unseen, in a long but brief fiery trail across the dark sky.

From the sky at night the land looks black, dotted by specks of light from the farmyard lights that pop on in rough unison when their sensors detect dusk. Here and there across the sprawling countryside stand intense clusters of lights in clean rows along the streets of towns where long-ago pioneers decided to stop and build a community. Now and then, a pair of lights moves out from these clusters along an unseen road toward another cluster.

In summer and fall this darkness is also punctuated by brief flashes of lightning that, for an instant, illuminate many miles of landscape to look like a colorless photographic negative. Seconds later comes the distant rumble of that sky-high spark that in one second moves more energy about the sky than a modern-day bomb. At any one time in the world five hundred thunderstorms are roaming about, distributing this energy and moisture and winds. At times these colossal columns of disturbed air are fifteen miles tall. At times they go crazy and become tornadoes that wreak havoc when their fingers of wind dip down to ground level. This helps explain why in many rural places across the nation's mid-section radio newscasts begin with the weather. At times these storms are full of sound and fury and no moisture whatsoever. Always, they are spectacles.

In contrast, the Mississippi River from up high at night looks quiet and black and much more twisting than from its surface. It wiggles like a giant worm in lazy, miles-long loops of geographic indecision east and west, even taking its mammoth flow back north a ways at times before inevitably falling south again. Off to both sides along the way are shorter, comma-shaped ribbons of black by the score, the oxbow lakes that were once part of a loop by the river's main channel until the corroding currents ate away at the banks sufficiently to cut those loops off forever and somewhat straighten the channel, momentarily at least. Such natural twists provide the most moisture to the maximum area. But they also have been responsible for transferring parts of one state into another without official permission.

And then comes a flash of unnatural light from somewhere around an upstream bend. It is an intense, incongruous illumination, coming as it does from amid dark woodlands or pastures of sleeping Holsteins. And this bright finger of light moves much quicker than anything else on the river—back and forth in short, staccato movements. Minute after minute, it grows brighter and brighter, actually brighter than bright, even still around the bend. Its beams turn a short stretch of river into broad daylight, bleaching away virtually all color save white and black. And its approach is accompanied by that now familiar powerful rushing sound of water.

Gradually, this light peeks around the bend, now turning this stretch of river into broad daylight. The creature resembles a towering, artificial Cyclops whose piercing gaze is grasped first by a fallen tree reaching out into the river, then by that buoy and the one across from it, then by an unusual pattern of ripples in mid-river, then straight down the main channel toward the next bend, then back and forth on both banks and dipping down toward its own feet. There, the white light reveals a gang of bulky towboat crewmen performing some nightly chore on the deck of this movable beast.

Despite the regularity of their passage, these creatures create an impressive and eerie spectacle. The light reveals to the captain all manner of warnings and helpful information on the river's changing conditions and personality as well as the presence of any other rivercraft and even lovers in cars parked on the numerous littered landings of mud that mark the passing riverbank. Another reason people still come down to the river is isolation and privacy, something not possible on, say, the interstate, where anyone not in a modern hurry attracts attention.

Less visible at night are the riverfront communities, tucked in behind their grass-covered levees or the fortresslike waterfront walls with their flying buttresses built to hold back the river before engineers began tinkering with changing the river's route itself. There is Columbus, Kentucky, where in 1927 for one hundred thousand dollars the Red Cross helped move what was left of the flooded community two hundred feet up the hill, where it stands today. In 1993, riverfront communities such as Valmeyer, Illinois, would still be making that same reluctant move up a hill to safety. Only nowadays, to move what was left of the town's three hundred forty-six homes, it cost more than sixteen million dollars.

While home to many, these river towns now are mainly minor glows in the midnight sky just over the treetops. They seem to have turned their backs on their decaying riverfronts and the adjacent waterway, although the sounds of Friday night football spill over onto the river. Motorists can travel for scores of miles along "riverfront" roads and never see the water, so hidden is it now by man-made walls. This obliviousness to the waterway, which drew these communities here in the first place, seems even more pronounced at night.

The low-lying homes in these river towns are no longer fancy; they're mainly just aging, their raised front porches and cellarless foundations speaking of a water wariness born from hard-earned, high-water experience. The dogs there, snoozing by the front door, no longer even bark at the approach of these rivercraft. Tricycles lie on lawns precisely where they were toppled this afternoon and where they will be joyously rediscovered tomorrow morning.

By midnight in such places the brightest light remaining downtown usually comes from the Miller sign in the lone tavern's dirty window or from the red glow of the Coca-Cola machine outside the darkened Standard Oil station. The old general store remains with a brick wall that still carries faded letters advertising an era when delivery boys carried groceries to customers' homes and phone numbers carried only four digits.

In some larger places, out by the highway intersection where homemade vegetable stands will soon sell the year's first ears of sweet corn, there stands the 1990s general store. It is an all-nite minimart charging inconveniently higher prices for the convenience of twenty-four-hour access to unleaded gasoline and leaded coffee, pre-packaged junk foods, prechilled six-packs, leather-skinned hot dogs, once fresh popcorn, creme-filled cupcakes barely clinging to six weeks of shelf life, and pre-mixed ravioli snacks in microwavable plastic cups. (No charge for the security camera surveying the scene from on high and photographing every customer every few seconds.)

As the towboat's finger of light rounds the bend by Hickman, Kentucky, it falls briefly on what appears to be a garishly lit, two-story, blue and white, floating minicity that gurgles loudly. It is impolite, according to river etiquette, to keep shining a spotlight on someone; it's kind of like staring. But even without the light's mega-wattage, it is clear that this river creature is a major installation.

It is, in fact, the *Natchez*, a powerful but helpless river dredge that cannot move itself but does move massive parts of the Mississippi's river bottom. It is privately owned but publicly contracted to the Army Corps of Engineers. For several months every summer on either side of Memphis, it ranges up and down the Mississippi and its tributaries, cleaning out harbors and shallows like a river Roto-Rooter.

Working twenty-four hours a day seven days a week, its powerful engines and lengthy hoses with bladed tips in effect vacuum up whole sandbars in the river and adjacent harbors and spit them out the back to dissipate, for now, into passing currents.

Some people might see dredge work as a drudge. Not Leland Olivier, who has spent about forty of his fifty-seven years cleaning out the Mississippi. His uncles and cousins dredged the same river. And they're all from—well, cook my shrimp—they're all proud Louisianans. If Louisiana had an application form for people desiring to live there, it would have two choices on birthplace: "Louisiana" and "Other."

Leland began as a deckhand, of course, for one dollar and five cents an hour. Today, he's deck captain of the *Natchez*, meaning he oversees the three crews of eleven men who work two weeks on and one week off wherever dredging needs doing. Come summertime they duck a little farther north. In winter, they pretty well stay below Memphis. The *Natchez* had arrived in Hickman forty-eight hours before from Mud Island down by Memphis. Leland figured sixteen days of dredging here, starting with the docks around Hickman's grain elevator where the river ferry doesn't run anymore. Then comes deepening the access to the rest of Hickman Harbor, which is a bit of a grand description for the brown backwater bend that curls past empty banks over toward town where the flood wall still stands sturdy, where Millard F. Carman is postmaster, and where the Fulton County High School Pilots will soon start practicing for another autumn's glory beneath Friday-night lights.

"This ole river is tricky," Leland says. "Some years it rises a lot, carries lotsa silt into harbors, and you need to dredge. Some years not. It all depends. This year is average. But we keep agoin—rain, sleet, or snow. The Corps has got

The River pretty well under control down here." That's the way many refer to the Mississippi—The River, like The Flag, The Corps, or The President, as if there's only one and everyone knows it. Or oughta.

Leland's daddy was a sugar, cotton, and sweet potato farmer down around Lafayette. Like a lot of young men in small towns, Leland thought, back in 1955, that he wanted to get away. He was right. He did. Ever since, he's spent two thirds of his working life away. Still, he's got seven kids—three girls and four boys, including one nuclear lab technician.

None of them works on the river. If they did, Leland would make darn sure they work better than the current generation of river workers. "They're from all over," he says, which means they're not from you-know-where. "They're not interested in the work," he says, waving across the din-filled deck. "They're just interested in the paycheck. They don't work as hard as we did, don't listen as good, and don't seem to have much ambition to work up in the system. It's damned hard to get good men now. And harder to keep 'em onct you do."

The *Natchez*'s whistle blows, summoning its tenders, a trio of mini-tugboats that shunt the dredge to the next set-up spot, not resembling *Show Boat* in the slightest. Time to move to the next sandbar. Leland touches his cap, the way deck captains used to on The River. He turns and, like every deck captain in history, starts yelling; once again, something is misplaced on a deck on the Mississippi River.

FIXES, FAXES, AND FEDEXES

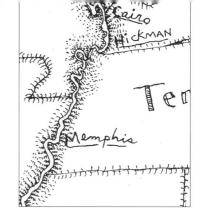

Despite its steady barge traffic, the section of the Mississippi River above Memphis emits an unexpected and powerful air of loneliness. It's like a grand old theater that opens every night although no one comes, not even the actors and actresses, just a lone dutiful usher now and then with no one to ush. At least abandoned railroad lines can be recycled into bicycle paths by yuppie suburban activists sporting goofy plastic helmets and, beneath their handlebars, neon water bottles filled with Evian. But what do you do with an old river that hasn't been Main Street for more than a century? It's these areas that produce the lonely memories that fuel an endless array of country music songs and a handful of hard-looking, hard luck folks who make a lucrative career singing them elsewhere. Indeed, Carl Perkins was born and raised in Tiptonville.

There are no roads, save for occasional levee pathways, that closely follow the riverbanks; at two million-plus dollars per mile, man-made roads tend to run much straighter than Nature's rivers. Some roads do dart off the main north-south highways several miles back and wander toward the river past frequent ponds, some aging houses with peeling paint and dirty dogs, tilting telephone poles whose wires are lined with hundreds of songbirds, and fertile farmfields dotted with occasional landing lanes for the seasonal flocks of crop dusters. But these narrow byways gradually decay, mile after mile, into pavement that crumbles, then dirt that's potholed, and end in a muddy, dim riverbank clearing circled by incestuous vines and littered with beer cans, spent fireworks, and stained Kentucky Fried Chicken boxes.

It is cooler in these clearings. And there is a real sense of history hanging about, though much of it seems overgrown. The New Madrid Earthquake, one of the largest ever to hit North America, rumbled through for a few weeks in 1811, killing few people because there were few there to be killed, but nonetheless altering the river's course and creating the thirty-nine-square-mile Reelfoot Lake.

The Civil War took somewhat longer to pass through. The struggle for this section of river was much less known than, say, the one regularly re-created and recaptured on film at Gettysburg or even the Siege of Vicksburg. It involved Union troopships sneaking downriver at night past Confederate emplacements and followed, come the next gray morning, by gunboats named *Cincinnati*, *Benton*, and *Pittsburgh*

towing barges with banks of mortars. The remains of seventy-five Confederate casualties from the battles of Madrid Bend and Island No. 10 are interred in a surviving country cemetery that is now part of the grounds of the Jones Chapel Church of Christ—VISITORS WELCOME MEMBERS EXPECTED. Another tiny headstone there, glistening in another gray summer drizzle, tells a sad story lost in time. It says simply: JAMES OTHEY BORN SEPT. 17, 1902 DIED DEC. 6, 1902.

Here and there, as if the river had become more of an obstacle than an artery, a huge bridge leaps over the water from one state to another. Now and then, a vehicle passes across, its tires humming incongruously in the countryside. If it's a truck or local resident's car, it speeds briskly across on its journey or errand to somewhere else. If the vehicle contains tourists, it may slow near midspan while the occupants try to peer over the eye level railing for a glimpse of the famous waterway. What they would see, if the bridge railing wasn't perfectly placed to obscure the view, is a river vista mostly empty save for a string of buoys pulling heavily against their chains in the strong, silent current.

The bridges are, of course, much busier when they cross at cities like Memphis, another one of those

Mississippi communities like Cairo whose location alongside a massive river suggested to Bible-reading white pioneers an ancient country in North Africa whose life is also dependent on a massive river.

Tennessee is greener than Egypt, forty-two thousand square miles nicknamed the Volunteer State for its record of military enlistments in the War of 1812 and the Spanish-American War. Tennessee is another one of those states where the flags of several rulers have flown—Spain, France, even North Carolina owned Tennessee for a while. Then, briefly, it was a state called Franklin, a territory, and finally, in 1796, the sixteenth state. The American Memphis is where two interstates—I-40 and I-55—now span the old-fashioned watery interstate and where, in 1541, a wandering Hernando de Soto looked out on the vast West and decided he had gone as far from Florida as necessary. Within that year, de Soto would be buried in that same river, a victim of malaria. Davy Crockett crossed the river there en route to his fate at the Alamo. The bridges off the Chickasaw bluffs at Memphis, as it happens, are also where Donna Green and Helen Grochowski saw the famous water for the first time. "This river is soooo big!" said Helen. This from someone born in Australia.

Both women are from Perth. They had long dreamed of touring the United States, especially the Grand Canyon and the Mississippi. They saved their money. They flew to Los Angeles. Now what? Well, it seems that many Americans love their own cars but are loath to spend the time driving across the country in them, having to look at all the extraordinarily ordinary sights in between the famous ones. So the Americans fly straight to their destination. No more time wasted on serendipity. Before leaving, they turn their cars over to a company that finds drivers. The company is paid by the car owners who get their cars delivered by drivers who get to see the sights for free. What a country!

Helen and Donna spent the entire summer crisscrossing North America in the cars of people they never met. They had allotted one and a half days in Memphis, just enough time to wade in Old Man River, to see The King's house, and to indulge in that traditional activity of tourists in America, buying T-shirts commemorating the experience. T-shirts are a relatively new but extremely profitable form of free speech. (It remains a mystery how the Roman Empire

Malcolm Burt, Beale Street, Memphis, Tennessee

lasted so long without toga shirts proclaiming: I CONQUERED GAUL AND ALL I GOT WAS THIS LOUSY T-SHIRT.

Malcolm Burt and his family have tapped into this American need to clothe oneself in colorful symbols and outrageous statements (RIVERBOATMEN DO IT IN BARGES). Years ago Malcolm's parents began selling roses from one street cart and then two. Street vending is a most lucrative business totally free of costs for rent, utilities, and other overhead. It is especially lucrative near office buildings around Valentine's Day right after quitting time as hurrying homebound spouses suddenly realize what day it is.

The Burts did so well in the street that they opened several other standard stores selling music and novelties. But Malcolm's franchise is the T-shirt trade on Beale Street. On every nice day and numerous cloudy ones the extremely jolly twenty-four-year-old can be found outside some blues club peddling his family's over-priced T-shirts.

He seems genuinely good-natured, genuinely interested in all passersby and in where they are from. "They're from everywhere except Memphis," he announces. "And everyone wants to know where the river is." Malcolm knows precisely where the river is (a few blocks west of his cart), a location he inevitably shares with the visitors after considerable good-natured bantering and even, at times, some bargaining that typically produces the sale of at least one T-shirt.

"I've always been a river person," Malcolm announces after hearing that one passerby is writing a book about the river. Malcolm says he virtually lived on Mud Island, which began as a sandbar that became an Indian settlement and, today, is a river museum (complete with a scale model Mississippi) at the end of an overhead monorail. "I fished down there," Malcolm adds. "I shot my BB gun down there. I took my school books down there."

What about dates? Did he ever take a girlfriend down to the river? "Maybe," Malcolm says, spying several T-shirts on his table that require urgent folding.

Downtown Memphis contains the usual platoon of tall, modern office buildings named for banks, where rents are higher on the river side, and the famous and opulent Peabody Hotel. The graceful old Peabody is home to America's most-photographed, most-coddled covey of ducks, who commute daily by elevator from their rooftop penthouse to their lobby pool.

The Memphis waterfront is a typical American urban setting—historic, often run-down, partly renewed with federal grants, hoping for more creeping gentrification, a place once vibrant with river life and the flourishing cotton trade. Some of the riverbank now is a daytime parking lot (in low-water times); it's still covered with the huge square stones that nineteenth-century cotton trade ships carried here as ballast and then discarded. Some of the bank is covered with the riprap stones used up and down the waterway to stabilize the earth next to moving water. Overlooking the banks now are some high-priced apartments marketing their downtown location and tranquil river views. And some of the bank is simply covered with mud and more modern refuse, which vagrants poke through when the begging business is slow.

Although trading and shipping cotton were important and Nashville became more famous for its country music, Memphis has long been a mecca for many musicians as well. Rivers have a wondrous way of inspiring music. "Old Man River," so tired of living and so scared of dying, seems to be about Memphis. Beale Street and W. C. Handy also perfected the blues there in the early 1900s. Then, in midcentury, in a tiny building called Sun Studios, a small, eventually famous assortment of artists began recording the songs that would revolutionize music. The Memphis sounds included and influenced many from Blues Boy (B. B.) King to Roy Orbison and Jerry Lee Lewis, from Johnny Cash and U2 to a now-deceased Mississippi truck driver who is still sighted around the country from time to time.

For Elvis Presley, like many Mississippians, Memphis, Tennessee, was the nearest big city and the Big Time. Even when his fame reached the outskirts of this galaxy, Elvis kept his home in Memphis; in fact, Graceland, out on Elvis Presley Boulevard, is the second most-visited celebrity home in America, after another white-porticoed house in Washington, D.C. And when Elvis died in Memphis, he was buried in Memphis, which overnight made Memphis a mecca for many pop music pilgrims, including Donna and Helen from Australia.

Such pilgrims number four and a half million every year, four times the Memphis metropolitan area's population, and their $1.6 billion in spending helps support 37,000 jobs. In recent years the city added to its attractions the National Civil Rights Museum, located not far from Beale Street in the old Lorraine Motel where Dr. Martin Luther King, Jr., was assassinated. Memphis is also semi-famous as the original home of Holiday Inns, the first Greyhound and Continental Trailways bus lines, and Piggly Wiggly, the first self-service grocery store, as well as Cybill Shepherd, Tim McCarver, and Volney, the late lion whose growl still announces the start of every MGM movie.

As computer technology, instant communications, overnight delivery, and jet travel eased the requirement for corporations to cluster in a handful of coastal cities, numerous noncotton companies moved to Memphis. They included Welcome Wagon, which found its welcome worn in New York City, where fearful residents have come to suspect women bearing gifts. But even fourteen decades after the steamboat's heyday, Memphis's importance for transportation lingers.

New Orleans aside, at night most Mississippi River cities grow quieter, the people on the streets fewer. Most parts of Memphis are like that, too. But southeast of downtown, a few thousand feet from the slow-moving barges on the somnolent Mississippi River, is another scene of impressive industrial choreography that reveals much about changing American tastes and methods.

There, in a brightly lit area the size of nearly three hundred football fields, several thousand employees nightly enact a high-speed, jet-age morality play worth millions of dollars to thousands of people preparing for bed all across the country and beyond the oceans.

As soon as the sky darkens, the planes of Federal Express, like immense aluminum birds returning to the nest, begin converging on Memphis. They appear from all directions, one after another. After another. After another. Radar tracks each. By the dozens, they fall into lines stretching several states away, descending in slow motion, feet down, headlights on, toward the lighted lanes of cement color-coded like river buoys. Each craft weighs several hundred thousand pounds.

They land delicately. They taxi awkwardly. One after another, they cross over, turn back and forth, en route to precise parking places set by computer and coached by pairs of long, colored flashlights waved in the dark by unseen human hands. The darkness's whirling din is high-pitched, whining, intense, full of eye-stinging fumes, and punctuated by horns and the white and red flashes of the planes' staccato strobe lights. Sounds swirl from all sides, like the brisk wind. So deafening is the arrival of these mechanical creatures that workers wear bulbous earmuffs for protection. To talk, they put their mouths by colleagues' ears, then shout, like the now-sleeping crew in the *Sumac*'s engine room.

Before the turbines' blades have stopped on the 727 at Gate 63, the plane's doors pop open, a posse of mini-tractors swarms in, and a message flashes from the clipboard computer of Michael Duncan on the ramp into the main hub computer a half mile away in front of Ken Tucker: Flight 216 has arrived from Greensboro, North Carolina. The number 216, which had been blue (not arrived) and then red (unloading crew assigned but plane not arrived), flashes to yellow (unloading under way). It is 11:23.

In 22.7 minutes, no record by FedEx standards, 216 will turn green (unloaded). Michael's Crew 17 has unloaded and moved onward more than forty thousand pounds of letters and packages in eleven steel containers. Each container carries a routing code, read by scanner as it is lowered from the plane. One container is rushed directly to the San Antonio flight. Two head for a 747 bound for Europe. Eight containers go inside for further sorting by hand and by computerized scanners along high-speed conveyor belts.

On this typical night between the first arrival, Flight 229 from Tampa at 10:35 P.M., and the last departure, 1650 to Omaha at 4:27 A.M., 4,600 FedEx workers will sort 704,424 packages out of 99 airplanes and 51 trucks back into 100 airplanes and 36 trucks. Quite some growth from that first night of FedEx's life, April 17, 1973, when 35 employees sorted 18 parcels on one card table. Since then, the brainchild of Fred W. Smith has spawned several competitors, changed the delivery expectations of a generation of Americans, and created a new verb, to FedEx, meaning to positively absolutely guarantee delivery tomorrow morning.

Fred Smith was an entrepreneur from Little Rock across the Mississippi in Arkansas. He had this idea that even the prefax pace of American life was quickening sufficiently to create a market out of Americans' deep-seated drive for instant gratification. Memphis was chosen as the main hub for its relatively central location, its empty hangar, and its fog-free weather. Subsidiary sorting hubs have since developed in Indianapolis, Chicago, Newark, Oakland, and Los Angeles.

Today, FedEx is by far the largest employer in Memphis, with 20,000 of its global 85,000 workers, many of them part-timers, who turn out nightly for a few hours sorting. Today, FedEx landings and takeoffs comprise nearly half the city's total air traffic. All traffic is FedEx after dark, which is great unless you're trying to sleep on a runway.

And more than seven hundred national catalog sales companies can promise their thousands of eager customers overnight FedEx delivery of everything from earrings to Christmas trees. Procrastinators can write their checks on the last day of the month and still make their payments on time. The last night of the month is always FedEx's busiest, although the volume every Thursday is always heavy, too, for letters, as businesses seek to consummate a week's work by week's end, and for flowers, chocolates, teddy bears, and lingerie, as suitors seek to smooth the way for weekend wooing.

But so hectic are those intense midnight hours that workers like Michael Duncan and the twelve co-members of his unloading team rarely know the origination city of any plane they're unloading. Michael is the son of a cross-country truck driver, transportation being one of the primary, lesser-skilled occupations that attract American workers displaced by crumbling rural economies. Michael is twenty-six years old, a former dairy department worker in a grocery store, from a small Mississippi town a fifteen-minute drive down the river where he goes boating, fishing, and waterskiing four or five times every summer week. Michael's home is, in fact, closer to the river than to work. And not by accident.

Moving goods and information for customers with more money than time has created a profitable market niche for air shippers, as well as for fax manufacturers. Time was Americans could wait two months for a letter to cross the country because they had to. Now they can't because they don't.

Michael was attracted to FedEx by the pay, the excitement, the competition among teams, and the company's benefits, which include free air travel to any of FedEx's one hundred nine cities. He's been to Wichita, Seattle, Las Vegas, and San Juan. Once, Michael got the idea to surprise an old college basketball pal in the District of Columbia. After work one night Michael boarded a 3:30 A.M. FedEx flight to Washington, arrived by 6:30, and spent the day with Fred Kramer sightseeing and shooting some hoops before flying back to Memphis at 10:30 the next night along with a few tons of outgoing government documents.

FedEx begins its daily cargo collections simultaneously with its morning deliveries. By late afternoon its fleet of four hundred smaller feeder planes is hopping across the country, picking up parcels and letters from smaller communities to deliver to its four hundred forty-four larger planes making their stops at the larger cities across the country and around the world. By morning, FedEx will have handled 1.4 million parcels all together, each of them computer-scanned seven times en route. It is one of those baffling facts of modern-day life (and federal regulations on interstate commerce) that a parcel can get across town in Phoenix faster and cheaper by going through Memphis. Too bad passenger airlines can't move people this well.

There is, too, a convenient commercial cachet that comes with the urgency of an overnight delivery. And it fits perfectly with the developing philosophy of inventory management "just-in-time delivery"; if you can get it here overnight, why bother tying up capital to maintain an expensive warehouse of parts?

The world of FedEx is a strange mixture of manual and high tech, composed of hundreds of lightning-wristed human letter sorters and handheld radios and scanners, computerized clipboards, and color-coded computer screens fed by the fleeting fingers of data processors. The human letter sorters aim for shooting fifty-five letters per minute into the appropriate slots; that earns them a seventy-cent-per-hour bonus.

The climate-controlled, central command room in Memphis is eerily silent, save for society's now familiar clicking of computer keys. Every two minutes the computer automatically totals how many parcels have been processed along the eighty-three computerized conveyor belts and projects a new finishing time. On this night, thanks to thunderstorms out West, the projected time was 2:30 A.M. versus an ideal time of 2:09.

The last plane drifted in at 1:15. The first one rushed out at 2:30, climbing up over the Mississippi on a diminishing trail of thunder.

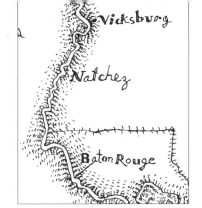

THE RIVER WITHIN

Below that plane and below Memphis the Mississippi River rolls silently and slowly on, moving along, on average, a little more than one mile every hour, about the pace of a strolling senior citizen. It has taken the river about 400,000 years to carve out the Upper Mississippi Valley down to Cairo, where it broadens some. Below Memphis, the Mississippi broadens greatly into a vast valley and then a delta that has been a conduit of creation for thousands of years. By Memphis, the river has fallen 775 feet since it began as a scenic brook trickling out of Lake Itasca; it still has 700 more feet to fall before its river journey ends far below New Orleans and its ocean journey begins.

The Mississippi Delta, it is said, begins on Beale Street. For millennia the Delta has been the beneficiary of billions of tons of silt ferried downstream by water and winds, grain by grain, to create a farm-fertile span of some of the continent's richest soils and poorest people sprawled across a potential floodplain two states deep and spanning more than one hundred miles of humid countryside. As recently as 3000 B.C. the bottom of the North American continent ended right around Baton Rouge. Since then, the Mississippi

River has moved and deposited enough of the Heartland downstream that Baton Rouge is two hundred twenty river miles from the Gulf of Mexico.

To spread its bounty even farther, the meandering river floods regularly, corroding its own overloaded banks, until one crevasses and the flow can burst through to sprawl over thousands of acres for a few weeks or months and deposit its lode of dirt. And, not confined in rock like the upper river, the lower Mississippi has changed its main course five times in the last fifty centuries. Its current path is about five hundred years old and would have changed again drastically by the mid-1970s, leaving Baton Rouge, New Orleans, and southern Louisiana as little more than muddy salt backwaters, were it not for the dams, gates, and hubris of river engineers. They shut off much of the shifting channel that had "stolen" 30 percent of the Mississippi's water by the 1950s. For the moment, modern engineering has frozen the Atchafalaya's borrowed flow at about one third of the Mississippi's water.

Just below Memphis, in Tunica County, Mississippi, nine more riverboat gambling casinos have emerged. Some are truly boats, others are maritime deviants, fixed structures defined as boats by landlocked regulators with eyes on revenues instead of rudders. By Greenville, Mississippi, the river is falling slower, about four inches for every mile. And then comes Vicksburg, where the Confederacy defied General Grant for a while and where the river acts obediently for a while.

Vicksburg (the Reverend Newitt Vick made a timely investment in one thousand acres of riverfront real estate just about the time steamboats arrived on the scene) is a graceful, sleepy, Southern community of thirty-three thousand, unjustly unfamous for being the place that Coca-Cola was first bottled. Until Joseph A. Biedenharn, a small-town candy merchant, got his pioneering packaging idea in 1894, thirsty Southern Baptists had to find a candy store to quench their desire for a nonalcoholic liquid beverage.

But Vicksburg is also a gentle reminder of the determining role that transportation has played in the urban history of America—with the location of urban development decided by river crossings, steamboat landings, railroad stations, and now interstate intersections and major airports. So important is the river still to Vicksburg life that hourly weather forecasts give the river's depth along with meteorological minutiae.

Given such importance even in the 1860s, Vicksburg, sitting atop the bluffs overlooking a gorge where the Mississippi plunges through, was seen as a crucial Union target. So Abraham Lincoln, one son of Illinois who had fought along the Mississippi during the Blackhawk Indian wars, sent Ulysses S. Grant, another riverfront son of Illinois, down the same Mississippi past Cairo, Madrid Bend, Island No. 10, and Memphis to reopen the Heartland's economic spine and pinch off the Confederacy from the West.

It was at Vicksburg, sitting astride his favorite horse, Cincinnati, which he named after another river city, that Grant focused the North's industrial might to refine his classical and ultimately successful siege strategy to destroy stubborn Southern strongholds. Such brutal effectiveness enhanced Grant's reputation, prompting an impatient Lincoln to make him overall Union commander. Leave it to General William Tecumseh Sherman to develop and refine the lightning-quick, scorched earth campaign strategy that, seventy years later, the Nazis would refine and call blitzkrieg. The unadorned Grant would surround a target, call it Vicksburg, Mississippi or Petersburg, Virginia, methodically sever every communications and supply link, and relentlessly pound such shrinking citadels until they surrendered. Not subtle, but effective.

Such a strategy worked better in military warfare than political warfare, as Grant was to learn five years later on the Potomac River after being crowned president by a grateful nation. Americans have a periodic infatuation with no-nonsense generals, beginning with Washington and running on through, among others, Jackson, Grant, Teddy Roosevelt, Eisenhower, and who knows who's next. (Sherman could have been in there, too, had he not announced he would not run if invited and would not serve if elected.)

It took Grant only forty-seven days from May 19, 1863, to subdue Vicksburg. It took Vicksburg eighty-two years to get over it; the Mississippi River even changed course, looping away from the city, before Vicksburg accepted defeat. Because the Northerners refused to accept Vicksburg's surrender until July Fourth, the city refused to celebrate July Fourth until 1945.

Today, the largest employer in Vicksburg is a federal agency, the Army Corps of Engineers' Waterways Experiment Station, a 4,286-acre installation that studies everything imaginable—and probably a few things that aren't. One of every ten Vicksburgians works at the research station on fifteen hundred projects from soil studies and blast effects to perfecting tank treads for different terrains and water flows. Prime among the station's topics is managing the lower Mississippi River.

Managing is a simple word. Put it next to the Mississippi River and it becomes considerably more complex, as Tom Pokrefke and Roger Saucier know only too well. They are among the unsung scientists of Vicksburg who spend endless hours studying rocks and mud, arrowheads and sand, moving water and the confetti they drop in to track the currents. The conclusions and theories of these men and their colleagues help shape the lives of millions of Americans—as well as the management and the future of this famous river.

The first efforts to control this waterway began long before the American Revolution, with the French in the early 1700s constructing levees (from the French *lever*, "to raise") to protect the site of New Orleans. Building a future Super Bowl site in a malarial swamp that sits below the surrounding water might seem an unlikely goal at first glance. Or even third glance. Despite the demonstrated success of the dike-building Dutch, who implemented the wheelbarrow more than six hundred years ago to help with that process, the early years in New Orleans saw much of that city regularly swept away by floods. To this day, it is not unusual to see ocean freighters sailing by above residential streets while dead New Orleans residents are still buried above ground.

But New Orleans controlled the mouth of the continent's most important river. Indeed, it was France's reluctance to allow midwestern Americans to conduct commerce through New Orleans that helped drive one of the largest real estate deals in world history, the Louisiana Purchase. This controversial purchase, which set in motion the acquisition of Florida, the annexation of Texas, the Mexican War, and the exploration, exploitation, and commercial conquest of a continent—not to mention setting the precedent for the purchase of Alaska—effectively doubled the geographic size of the United States. Until the Louisiana Purchase, the Mississippi River was the United States' western boundary.

Soon after, the nation turned to the Corps of Engineers, a cadre of construction experts produced by the country's only engineering school, the U.S. Military Academy at West Point. Once confined to fort-building, the

Corps was reinvigorated and assigned the task of surveying and then unsnarling the Heartland's rivers, long clogged with sandbars and natural jumbles of trees, a few such snarls up to thirty miles long. Private anti-flood levees of dubious structural integrity also were going up along the river. In the mid-nineteenth century, Congress passed the Swampland Acts, awarding to the states swamplands adjacent to the river. These were pre–Environmental Impact Statement days, before anyone doing anything that might affect anywhere had to write, rewrite, and then re-rewrite a vast, multi-volume EIS detailing every single conceivable effect of the project, except how many forests were felled to make the paper for so many copies of a report read by so few people.

The swampy areas adjacent to the river were leveed, drained, and then sold to plantation owners to produce cotton and other crops, including property taxes. Land sales proceeds went toward the next levee. Following several major floods this century, including the devastating 1927 flood, the federal government took a more activist, long-term anti-flood role, investing billions in water impoundment areas on Mississippi tributaries, immense bank stabilization schemes,

levees that now line virtually every inch of the Mississippi's western bank from Cape Girardeau to the Gulf, and huge floodways, which are, in effect, backup riverbeds for peak periods. This prevented many billions more in flood damage. "People forget," says Dr. Michael C. Robinson, the Corps Division Historian in Vicksburg, "the regular dread and irregular devastation that Mississippi floods spread across the land every year."

It was one thing to float flatboats downstream laden with farm produce, as many pioneers did, including one A. Lincoln. The rafts or even keelboats could be disassembled and sold for lumber in New Orleans. Others were pulled, poled, or winched back upstream against the current and lurking river pirates.

The advent of steamboats came in 1811 when the *New Orleans,* a thirty-eight-thousand-dollar joint venture of Robert Livingston and Robert Fulton of Hudson River steamboat fame, chugged out of Pittsburgh on September 24 and pulled into Natchez on Christmas Eve. The arrival of steamboats made river navigation a priority. Early on, the Spanish had actually sailed up the Mississippi as far as what became Vicksburg. But they had good sailors. Better yet, they had slaves to row.

Steamboats constituted more than just a passing spectacle and romantic chapter in history. They were essential to inland commerce, carrying settlers in and produce out. Old photographs show some craft so stacked and laden with cargo, the boats looked more like moving mountains of cotton bales with a pilothouse peeking out. By the Civil War, about one thousand steamboats plied the Mississippi carrying, by one estimate, more cargo each year than the entire British commercial fleet.

Along with the developing telegraph and railroads, Mississippi River steamboats were an important and perhaps the last, most picturesque step in the inexorable quickening of American life. Where it had taken six months to pole a keelboat from New Orleans back up to Ohio, steamboats came to do it in six days. This was deemed progress. And what red-blooded American would ever dare to oppose progress?

The north-south steamboat traffic gave way to gunboat traffic during the Civil War, civilian travelers being understandably more desirous of being passengers than targets. The steamboat culture resumed after the unpleasantries and even flourished into the early 1900s before giving way to today's more utilitarian metal barges and the gawdy gambling boats en route to nowhere.

But all the while navigation remained essential, navigation on the Mississippi meaning a reliably navigable channel at least nine feet deep. This was when and where science slowly entered and the realization grew among river handlers that controlling the Mississippi was an unrealistic goal. Training might be a better word.

For while the Mississippi, from a distance, looks like a river, up close and down under, it is actually several rivers, most of them potentially lethal to interlopers. And each of them is a combination of dynamic natural and unnatural forces, constantly changing and reacting to each other.

Tom Pokrefke noticed this as a child growing up in the countryside just outside St. Louis in what is now, of course, a suburban housing development. He and his pals played regularly in a nearby stream, which was great fun unless you were responsible for little Tom's laundry. The boys constructed little dams, grew pools of tadpoles, launched endless fleets of stickboats with leaves for sails, and bombed them with dirt balls. Tom noticed then how the dirt dissolved in the water and seemed to swirl and how sometimes some things did not move directly downstream. Amid all the downbound water, a floating leaf, a sunken stick, or some silt might actually head back upstream a ways. He thought nothing about that. Today, he knows better.

In college, Tom figured to become a mechanical engineer. However, on registration day the line was so long at that table that he signed up for civil engineering instead. Today, he is chief of the River Engineering Branch at the Waterways Experiment Station in a cluttered office with a squeaky chair off a hallway lined with pictures of the gods of engineering—Isaac Newton, Giovanni Battista Venturi, and others. And he tries, with the impressive patience of a real river watcher, to explain the dynamics within a river.

"A river is always changing," he says with enduring enthusiasm. "Every second. Everywhere. Water is a volume. So is silt. They each move at different speeds. And each moves differently when mixed. Say you have a high volume of water that undercuts a bank, causing a tree to fall in. The presence of that dirt and that tree will affect the river's flow. Now you have things like this happening on both sides

every inch of the way from Minnesota to the Gulf.

"Clear water flows differently than silt-laden water. Sediment makes a given volume of water meander more. And as it meanders, it's constantly picking up sediment and dropping sediment, changing its character at each moment. Now, different levels of water within the same river move at different speeds because they have different loads. Some are moving along in layers, higher velocity water on top. Some are turbulent, mixing with each other and changing each other's load and speed. Look, here's a plot of a velocity meter stuck in the river. Over ten minutes, the water velocity averaged four feet per second. But look at the speeds. They vary from ten feet per second to one and a half feet per second, even within a river that looks pretty calm on the surface.

"Now, to avoid choking itself to death, this river has to move basically two things from the Rocky Mountains through the Midwest to the Gulf of Mexico. It's got to move bedload, that is, material—perhaps pea-sized stones—moving along on or near the bottom. Now remember, each pea-sized stone was once part of an egg-sized stone that was once part of a melon-sized stone that was once part of a stone the size of this desk that was once part of a stone the size of a truck that once fell off the side of a mountain. It has gone through God-only-knows how many freeze-thaw cycles that break it down, and the water and the tumbling has chipped off pieces and smoothed each piece down to your familiar river stones.

"And the river has also got to move its suspended load, all the fine silts and clays it picks up along the way from farms in Kansas and trees that fell in Illinois. A little stone in the bedload could take one thousand years to move fifty miles. A grain of silt could leave Kansas in May and get dumped in the Gulf come fall. More likely, it would take many years to float a ways, then fall out a while, then float a ways, then fall out.

"That suspended load pretty well stays in the system all the time. As some is dumped in the Gulf, more is carried away from Kansas. And that load can change over time as, say, land use changes. Or you build one dam. That affects the silt load. It may take fifty years to clean out the system, but eventually the water will move all its suspended load downstream. We've noticed a decline in the silt load due, among other things, to better farming practices since the 1930s. That's good for the river. But it's not so good for the Delta. Deprived of so much new silt, the Delta is shrinking every year.

"Now, what we've done essentially from Cairo to the Gulf is turn the Mississippi into a good flood control channel. We use levees to keep it contained. And we use bank stabilization—really just concrete blankets laid on banks where the river wants to eat away—to prevent more meanders. That reduces the load of silt to be moved or dropped in the channel, enabling the water to move faster. The other thing was back in the thirties we cut off a couple dozen of the larger meanders, just let the river go straight south instead of twisting back and forth for miles. Nature abhors straight lines. But that saved upwards of one hundred fifty miles of travel for barges and it meant more water could be moved faster at flood times. But that also means less room in the river to store water. So it takes less water to have a flood. And faster water up here causes more scouring problems down there.

"See, if mankind was running the show, every time we put one unit of silt in at the top, we'd move one unit of silt out the bottom. But nature works on eternity, not eight-hour shifts. The river is moving different loads at different speeds in different places at different times. It backs up. For instance, up at Lock and Dam 26, which my grandfather—he was a pipefitter—helped build back in 1935. Well, up there, seventy-five percent of the silt moves twenty-five percent of the time. That means most of the silt moves in the spring, and the rest of the time it just sits there.

"You can't see it, of course, but the river bottom is constantly being sculpted by the currents moving at different speeds with different loads. In places, it's flat. In places, it's like waves of sand and mud building up to ten, maybe fifteen feet high along the bottom, then eventually falling down into the next gully and building another wave, on and on all the time, moving a few feet or inches now, and then sitting a while. In the lower Mississippi, we can get sandwaves as tall as thirty feet. The Coast Guard spots 'em on the fathometer. But since they're under one hundred feet of water, who cares?

"Now, in high water, the current will move the load out of this area in a bend and drop it down here. In low water, it'll drop it in the bend and wash it away down there. But remember, the river's velocity varies from side to side and top to bottom. So it's building a wave here, destroying the same wave there, and flushing it clean right there to move the material and make another wave down here.

"And on and on it goes from the surface to the bottom, from Minnesota and Montana to the Gulf."

This is, of course, far too great a scale for humans to grasp at once, even with satellite photographs. So what the engineers have done, literally, is scale down the Mississippi for study. Beginning more than a half century ago, forty miles east of Vicksburg, near Jackson, Mississippi, the Corps constructed a scale model of the entire Mississippi River drainage system, all 1.25 million acres and 15,000 miles of rivers of it, on eight hundred acres of government land. It is one historic measure of the political and economic importance attached to studying and trying to control the Mississippi River that such a gargantuan domestic project was undertaken in 1943, right in the middle of World War II. Much of the initial construction work was done by three thousand German POWs, mostly members of General Rommel's famed Afrika Korps.

In a matter of minutes this complex irrigation project could be used to recreate the Flood of 1927 or any past or potential inundation. If rains dump a sudden six inches of moisture on Omaha, what does that mean for the level and levees at Memphis? With one day equaling five point four minutes of flow on the model, weeks of study and prediction could be made in only hours.

In recent years, as part of the ongoing disassembly of the vast empire of federal installations across the country, the Mississippi scale model at Jackson was closed and parts turned over to the city for a park. But back in Vicksburg, under a roof, engineers constructed another scale model of Mississippi River sections that pose regular management problems. It was there a few years ago, sitting on a ladder laid over the pretend river, his feet dangling not far from the surface, that Tom Pokrefke noticed something. Contrary to popular belief, the exclamation "Eureka!" is not a part of scientists' everyday vocabulary. It's more like a quiet, "I wonder what would happen if . . ."

Tom had seen the real Dogtooth Bend. Now he studied the scale model Dogtooth Bend for countless hours. If he wasn't a patient person by trade, he would be by family; Tom has four children. So he studied Dogtooth Bend for countless hours. That bend is a perennially and particularly troublesome chunk of river twenty miles above Cairo, just below Thebes, where the upper Mississippi is about to break out of its narrowness, and Chief Morris and the *Sumac*'s buoy patrol move through every two weeks. Dogtooth was so much trouble that virtually every year the Corps had to hire Leland Olivier and his dredging colleagues to scoop it out.

Bends are always trouble for barge navigation. Water flowing around a river bend flows slowest on the inside curve and fastest on the outside curve. It's much like a line of children holding hands and playing the old crack-the-whip game; the children closest to the swing point can move slowest, while youngsters on the far end must run to keep up. The river tends to deposit silt on the inside of the bend, narrowing the navigation channel further. At the same time the river tends to scour the outside parts of the bend, creating new meanders and adding more dirt load to the same amount of river water to be carried downstream to be deposited and moved ad infinitum.

For hours, like some little boy playing in a country creek, Tom would sit on the catwalk over the scale model Dogtooth Bend, watching. For the uninitiated, watching a scale model Mississippi River is rather like watching paint dry. Every so often Tom would sprinkle a few pieces of paper confetti into the water to see where the upper currents took them.

The scale model's river bottom is covered with crushed coal, which acts like river sand. Predictably, Tom could see the internal currents slowly piling the grains on the bend's inside corner and scouring away others from the outside. Underwater walls have long been used to steer river currents. James B. Eaves, a self-trained nineteenth-century engineer who built the ironclads and the first steel bridge at Memphis, had shown how underwater jetties—walls of stone built essentially parallel to the channel—could somewhat confine the flow to increase its strength. This steered the river's own currents naturally and continually to flush sand and silt from the river's mouth to keep the river channel deep enough for oceangoing ships to navigate up to New Orleans and beyond.

Tom Pokrefke and his team played with that idea. It's not unlike the principle of a snow fence, disrupting air or water currents sufficiently to cause them to drop their cargo away from a highway or river channel while allowing other currents to blow or flow through freely. The Vicksburg engineers built jetties, scale-model underwater walls, parallel to the channel. And then they built some walls, called dikes, perpendicular to the channel. Underwater dikes are used to improve navigation by increasing water depth in the main channel. Some two hundred twenty miles of dikes have been built out of sight within the lower Mississippi. Their use has been so refined that some dikes contain notches to direct part of the current to gouge out depressions to improve riverbottom fish habitat.

Then Tom wondered what would happen if the walls were built angling slightly upstream, instead of perpendicular to the bank. They built a few in the model. Something strange happened. So they did it again. And again. And again. It still happened.

The confetti on the upper layer of moving river water still floated around the bend the same way. But if you watched closely—and Tom and his crew did watch very closely—they saw the downbound undercurrents now picking up the grains of crushed coal from the inside of the bend and depositing them on the outside. That is exactly the opposite of what the river normally does. And it is exactly what river managers would like a well-behaved river to do. In effect, the underwater walls, called bendway weirs, fool the river into thinking the bend goes the other way.

So now the river's own currents not only widen the channel in the bend, they add weight to the outside riverbank, also a plus for river management. Further study showed that the weirs also smoothed out currents through the bend, eliminating treacherous pockets of turbulence that navigators have feared since before Samuel Clemens was a pilot apprentice. And these underwater benefits continued some distance downriver, too, in a kind of watery echo effect.

Some people think of riverbanks as walls. Hydraulics engineers and river managers know they are more like continuous teeter-totters. If the weight of the passing river is greater in any one spot than the bank along that same spot, the water will move under the bank and tip it into the river. River settlers knew the phenomenon, if not the hydraulics principles; that's why for centuries, since early Roman times along the Po,

they've been weaving huge mats of willow branches and sinking them with large stones along the outside of so many river bends facing the river. Of course, denuding river banks of handy trees that also helped hold soil in place did little to improve the erosion situation.

So that isn't done anymore. At low water on the Mississippi, the Corps now accomplishes the same thing with strips of cement wired together into folding blankets the size of football fields. The correct kind of cement even encourages algae to grow on it to feed river fish.

Now Tom had discovered that the river could be trained to add weight to its own outside riverbanks while flushing its own main channel more reliably. As one result, over the course of several years, the Corps built twenty-five bendway weirs, each about thirty-five feet tall and eight-hundred feet long, along a couple of miles of Dogtooth Bend. Remember that load of rock that the *Bethany Dawn* was pushing downstream one morning when the *Sumac* met it off Cape Girardeau? Those rocks were destined to be dumped in Dogtooth too, where they now reside, out of sight, silently steering the currents of this ancient waterway.

*   *   *

When we can find the time, one of the most mesmerizing aspects of watching the Mississippi River—indeed, of watching much of Nature—is its total disregard for time, as measured by clocks, anyway. Mankind and womankind run around fussing over the passage of time or the saving of some. Every day everyone is in a major hurry and behind from the start of the instant breakfast. Even some new songs are introduced as "future golden oldies." Then we fib about or fog over our ages, as if by coyly declining to say the accurate number of our fleeting years we somehow suspend their passage.

Throughout history much of our human ingenuity from the invention of the wheel, the messenger pigeon, the steam and gasoline engines, chain saws, and the airplane to phones, FedExes, faxes, pagers, voice mail, and microwaves (plus all the thinking that has gone into all the advertising that tries to train all of us to think we need a faster-working nasal decongestant and antifungal foot liniment), all of this ingenuity and imaginative prowess has been invested in condensing time. As if there was only so much time flying toward us through space.

We sometimes seek to sit in the awesome presence of such an elemental natural force as a river or a mountain. Something that, unlike so much of our own making and choosing, has been there since before us and will be there long afterward. Something powerful and apart that does not respond to a remote control. Some cultures have even made mountains and rivers into deities because through them, humans somehow absorb a soothing inkling of forces much larger, grander, and far more everlasting than our puny, passing selves. Something better even than virtual reality, though admittedly lower scoring. So it is for many individuals who study the historical and physical phenomenon of this river.

One such individual is Roger T. Saucier, Ph.D. He's a New Orleans native, about sixty years old, tall and gangly still, the product of a broken home before they were so numerous and required study by social scientists. He pretty much raised himself, Roger Saucier says, quietly. Quiet things have a way of being overlooked more easily these days. Overpowered, actually. In an era of four hundred channels, Walkmans, and digitalized Dolby Sound, when Geraldo Rivera, Howard Stern, Rush Limbaugh, and John McLaughlin's crowd carry on society's daily dialogues, loudness wins, especially smart-ass loud. It's not what you say that builds credibility over time and stimulates a video-numb audience to stay tuned and maybe even listen as well. It's how you say it, and how quickly. Loud is good. Louder is better. Quiet doesn't sell well to people who think well-read means being up-to-date on *People* cover stories. Can you imagine Dr. Albert Schweitzer on the David Letterman show? That's what I mean.

Yet, somehow, quiet survives in some corners, quietly. Much about Dr. Saucier is quiet—his pale blue slacks, plain black belt and even paler blue-checked shirt (short-sleeved) with the silver pen and matching spare waiting obediently in the breast pocket. No-nonsense graying hair still styled in a crewcut. Eyeglasses that quietly darken to sunglasses. He stands and walks with his arms behind the back, hands clasped, confidently, humbly, thoughtfully, like a strolling prince who need not shout to be heard.

Such quiet men are also meticulous about what they say, and most meticulous about what they do not say. It's as if each of Dr. Saucier's words are the stroke of a soft brush whisking away grains of sand on the site of an archaeological dig on some isolated hillside to reveal his intended meaning. With each word invested with so much thought, meaning, and enthusiasm, people tend to listen closely.

As a boy, this man was intrigued by archaeology, riding his bicycle alone at first then later with friends out into the southern Louisiana countryside in search of ancient Indian campsites and the debatable secrets they held.

It's hard to describe the quiet excitement, the blood rush that comes with unearthing a fragment of an old clamshell. Then another and another. And others. A regular little mound of them. Maybe the campfire was over there; if it's large, that might mean the climate here was not as warm back then as Louisiana's tourism folks tout today. An animal-skin shelter may have stood nearby. And, look, a stone projectile point! With a familiar style—see that little depression ground in to make the arrow fit better on a spear? And this point is a whopper! They weren't hunting rabbits with this baby. The family probably squatted around here, smashing the clamshells and eating their chewy contents, unaware of the dramatic tale of ancient routine that their dinner detritus would tell one hundred centuries later.

William McIntire, the geographer, saw promise in this Saucier fellow. Got him a student job at Louisiana State University, where Roger studied geology and geography, also anthropology and archaeology. He's spent much of his career as a bridge, using geology and archaeology to help the other. In effect, this stepson of an insurance salesman turned Coast Guard civil servant is a reconstructor of the past through physical links with the present. A modern-day Indiana Jones without the hat, jacket, whip, gun, glamour, drama, or blonde. And forget the Nazis, too.

The Corps calls him a physical scientist. "To me," Dr. Saucier says carefully, "geology or geography is like a fascinating intelligence game. Intelligence in the military sense. To me, it is a constant challenge to understand how natural processes have worked and what those natural processes have created. And then, to me, it is particularly fascinating to tie man into all of it. Albeit prehistoric man.

"See, up north the glaciers erased everything. So some of the best evidence we have of what has happened is in the Mississippi Valley. Much of the evidence has come about by examining locations where the Indians lived, the conditions they lived under. We can determine what streams were probably active at the time, what streams were abandoned. We have learned so much about thousands of years just in the last twenty years.

"We've learned, for instance, that what we thought we knew is not correct: We once thought the Ice Age began about a million years ago. Now, we believe it was more like two million when the first sequence of glaciers began their advance. There were four major advances and four major retreats. But nothing is that simplistic in nature. The advances and retreats were not clean steady things. They'd advance a few centuries and then retreat several hundred miles and then advance again. From beginning to end, each cycle might last one thousand centuries.

"They'd start up in Canada around Hudson Bay and to the east with other lesser centers elsewhere. Some years they'd hardly move, others they'd move tens of feet in a year, scraping up anything loose in their path, gouging out the Great Lakes, deepening valleys, and nudging all the debris ahead. The Canadian Shield is basically bedrock scraped clean by grinding glaciers. When they'd retreat, the glaciers would sometimes leave their debris in lines. They're called moraines. Long Island is a moraine, probably rocks and soil nudged down from Quebec.

"That same glacier, called the Laurentide Ice Sheet, was the last big one. It started, oh, about twenty-seven or twenty-eight thousand years ago in Hudson Bay. In ten thousand years it grew down to Long Island, across northern Pennsylvania, dipped down pretty much just north of the present Ohio River all the way to the Mississippi just above Cairo. There's a group of hills there that didn't get flattened.

"The glacier crossed the Mississippi then, covering the northern half of Illinois, part of Wisconsin, and angling northwest into Minnesota, then dipping back down in a lobe into Iowa and pretty much following the Missouri River west and northwest and leaving the United States in North Dakota. The remnants of that one didn't fully disappear in Canada until nine thousand or ninety-five hundred years ago. That was a short one though, only eighteen thousand years long. The one before was more like sixty thousand years long. It ended at least one hundred twenty thousand years ago. It's hard to know for sure since the previous traces were erased up north by later glaciers."

Down south, it is easier to track the changes, studying the layers of windblown silt, or loess, and waterborne silt. With so much of the world's moisture locked up in the snow and ice of glaciers, the sea level dropped by perhaps one hundred meters, inviting across the Bering Strait into North America the hunters of both continents' wildlife—of the mammoths and llama-, pig-, and horse-like creatures. The easiest way to move across a forested countryside was to follow a riverbed. It was open. There was water and food. Humans weren't the first species to build their communities along waterways. And paths up a riverbank were excellent spots for both animals and humans to ambush each other.

But the glacier's lockup of so much of the earth's water also initiated the new, slowly changing weather patterns and cyclical droughts that created the glaciers' own demise, allowing more snow to melt each year than fell. "Man isn't doing anything to nature that nature hasn't already done," Roger observes. "But we do accelerate the process."

The glaciers also created their own cold climate,

Roger Saucier, geographer, environmental laboratory,
U.S. Army Corps of Engineers, Vicksburg, Mississippi

including fierce winds that moved massive amounts of soil all over the Heartland and down the Mississippi Valley, creating a massive prehistoric Dustbowl. Using palynology, Roger and others can reconstruct rough pictures of that prehistoric landscape. Palynology is basically studying pollen grains, those minute powders that irritate sinuses. Thousands of years ago, those grains settled on the ground and were buried in bogs as clues for future detectives.

These grains tell informed eyes what ancient vegetation flourished where. "We know now," Roger notes, "that during the last period of maximum glaciation, about twelve to eighteen thousand years ago, the vegetation out on the Mississippi's alluvial plain as far south as Baton Rouge contained species like larch, fir, and spruce, boreal species like those now found around the upper Great Lakes and southern Canada and the Mississippi's source. The climate was cool enough and wet enough that those species could survive this far south. The year-round average temperature was probably no more than five degrees cooler than today. That's all it takes."

The river was flowing differently back then. It wasn't today's familiar meandering river pattern, with a central flow zigzagging across a valley floor. It was more like the flow from an immense clogged shower head, a miles-wide system of shallow, independent, braided channels, sometimes running parallel to each other, sometimes crossing over each other, running together a while and then splitting apart. The braids were constantly changing and ran roughly parallel downstream perhaps fifteen or twenty miles across the valley floor.

"Here at Vicksburg today," Roger says, "the Mississippi meanders but really has a rather well-defined channel, albeit a very dynamic one. Normally, the river here is about forty feet deep and at floodstage maybe a hundred feet deep and about a mile wide. But when the glaciers were melting, the channels were probably ten to fifteen feet deep. And at any one point in the valley, you'd have maybe fifteen of them side by side, all active simultaneously. And each could have been a few thousand feet wide."

When the glaciers were melting, data indicates the Mississippi's annual spring runoff was ten times the size of today's. Someone writing a book on the Mississippi River might think to ask Dr. Saucier a simple question: What data on the river from eighteen thousand years ago?

"I'm glad you asked," he says, warming to this glacial epic. "We cannot know empirically a river's flow back then. Or which braids were active when. But we have dug up some evidence from the Gulf of Mexico.

"That evidence consists of either microscopic or near-microscopic organisms that have lived in the Gulf's deep waters. Living organisms will contain different types of isotopes of elements, including oxygen. By looking at the ratio of these various isotopes like oxygen twelve and fourteen, we can determine how cold the Gulf water was. And by knowing how cold the water was, we can extrapolate the volumes of incoming fresh water it would have taken to make those temperature conditions in the larger Gulf. By mathematical modeling, we can then say that a certain volume of water at a certain temperature flowed south."

Dr. Saucier sits back in his chair, rather pleased. Elementary, my dear Watson.

The meltwater back then was volumi-nous and powerful enough to carry along gravel. As the glaciers disappeared and the runoff dwindled, the size of the river's cargo of dirt dwindled too. The pebbles grew fewer and smaller. The silt was more predominant. In the last century, especially the last sixty years, as the Corps and landowners grew more experienced in their battles against erosion—redirecting currents, channeling a river prone to wander, lining vulnerable areas of riverbank, and damming the Upper Mississippi—even the volume of that cargo diminished. As one result, the Mississippi River Delta below New Orleans is not being fed silt and fresh water as it once was. Nothing stays static in Nature. So just as glaciers deprived of new moisture start to shrink, the river Delta has been similarly deprived and continues to shrink, too. The ocean's salt water continues to encroach and the Delta's marshlands are dwindling every year by about twenty-three square miles, almost fifteen thousand acres.

The nuclear reactor run by Systems Energy Resource, Inc., Grand Gulf, Mississippi

Wayne Stroupe, public affairs officer of the Waterways Experiment Station, Vicksburg, Mississippi

Evening traffic, Natchez, Mississippi

The Mississippi Basin Model, Jackson, Mississippi

Kids boarding the ferry, Pointe a Le Hache, Louisiana

Billy Hingle, ferry captain, Pointe a Le Hache, Louisiana

Grain elevator, Laroche, Louisiana

Earl Hingle on the porch of one of his houses, Ostrica, Louisiana

Earl Hingle, Donald Hingle, and customer in the general store, Buras, Louisiana

Pilottown, Louisiana

Pilottown, Louisiana

The *Red Snapper* at her final mooring, Ostrica, Louisiana

A tanker heading for the Gulf

The *Golden Polydamnos* moving up the Mississippi

Looking back at the Mississippi from the Gulf of Mexico

Dawn over the mouth of the Mississippi

THE BOTTOM

Wayne Stroupe and Jim Slavens have just about absolutely nothing in common—except their love for the Mississippi River and the way they feel when they're on it. Jim, you'll remember, is that riverboat banker from up in Davenport.

And Wayne, well, Wayne's his own piece of work. He's the kind of person who, come Christmas time, would set up a Santa sleigh in his front yard (remember now, this is Mississippi) pulled by eight pink lawn flamingoes. One year someone, obviously with good taste, stole the flamingoes. The story got on the television news. Within days, Wayne's lawn was covered with pink flamingoes donated by strangers who had been unable to have theirs stolen.

Wayne is one of the many civilians who work for the Army Corps of Engineers in Vicksburg. That keeps him in groceries, near the river, and working on river studies. But unlike Jim Slavens, Wayne has had nothing to do with banks, except for the mortgage on the twelve-thousand-five-hundred-dollar boat he takes with him most everywhere like a wallet. "That boat," he says, using the intentional grammatical misspeak that men employ to make a strong assertion go down easier among friends, "don't ever leave without me being on it."

Not that any inexperienced innocent from away should ever seek to tackle river navigation alone without a river veteran. Wayne is a veteran. He dreams of someday starting a tourism-related business, maybe his own marina or restaurant excursion boat, that would enable him to work on the river and get paid. For now, he must settle for warm week nights and weekends. "I don't mind sweating like a feverish demon," he says, "but I sure don't want to shiver ever again."

More Saturdays and Sundays than not, Wayne dodges the new gambling casinos downtown to back his pride and joy into the muddy waters that gently lift his eighteen-foot Wellcraft off the soft cushions of the trailer. In the water of Wayne's world, with its one-hundred-fifty-horsepower Yamaha engine rumbling deeply, Wayne's boat seems far lighter than its twenty-five hundred pounds.

He eases out into the river and then, with a sly smile, guns the boat upstream where it bounces from wave to wave, slamming into some waves with the impressive force of a fullback colliding with a linebacker. Wayne might go for a picnic lunch on a sandbar or a high-speed cruise, or both, followed by a massive onshore meal of catfish, greens, corn bread, and beer. Along the way, over the roar of the engine, Wayne points out good fishing spots, the ripples that warn of shallow water, and the "blue logs," those sodden tree trunks that have been downbound for years, just below the surface. There are no dams on the Lower Mississippi to filter out such debris.

A mile or two above Vicksburg, he cuts the engine and points out over the smooth, seemingly safe water. Up close, the water is covered with countless swirls that speak of underwater currents. Two minutes later, just for a few seconds, an immense boil of water erupts audibly, several feet across, the surface indicator of grand turbulence far below amid the competing currents of the surface river and the bottom river. An unsuspecting waterskier hitting that could be sucked under so easily. Then Wayne cruises down beneath the bridge, slowing to point out the ancient stone pillars gnawed by the rushing currents. Yellow, brown, red, and even green scars tell of past encounters with even slightly wayward downbound barges. So hard and fast do the currents push against these old pillars that the water level seems several feet higher on the upbound side.

Sometimes, especially on those early summer weekends when Wayne still appreciates the newly arrived warmth, he blasts off downriver himself. It's quicker, of course, to haul the boat down the road—about a three-hour drive to New Orleans and maybe another two hours to the river's mouth. Free time seems to come in more bite-size chunks in America on the eve of the new millennium. But if Wayne had vacation time that could be measured in several days, he'd no doubt take his boat downriver in the river to the vast Gulf. There, so many speckled trout and redfish await their fate at the end of Wayne's fishing line and in his frying pan at a familiar rented fishing camp. Now, don't that just set your idle mind to thinking and your mouth to watering?

This is the last long leg of the river's journey from the woods of northern Minnesota to the watery wilds of the Gulf. The Mississippi has long since lost its innocence and purity on this transcontinental trek. That came well before the river entered the chemical alley of Baton Rouge, now so tightly lined with nearly one hundred petrochemical industries—refineries, factories, storage tanks, freighters, and tankers—just between Baton Rouge and noisy New Orleans, now increasingly populated with casinos and the people who flock to these false economic panaceas.

There is even another interior river struggle under way at New Orleans. As the world's sea level rises and more water is taken from the Mississippi, including the drinking supplies for one third of all Louisiana, the river's flow is reduced in volume and gradient. Hydraulically, this virtually invites the ocean to fill the vacuum. In recent years, river engineers like Tom Pokrefke detected vast volumes of the heavier salt water creeping upstream within the Mississippi River's banks beneath the two layers of downbound fresh water. The salt water not only threatened the river's freshwater ecosystem. It also threatened the drinking water supplies for numerous communities, including New Orleans.

More studies on that river model in Vicksburg suggested a solution. And it worked. The Corps built a series of underwater dams, some thirty feet tall, all across the river bottom. Unseen far beneath the passing hulls of freighters that cruise along the leveed river above the main streets of riverside communities, these underwater dams, or walls, blocked the upstream movement of the ocean while permitting the downstream movement of the river and its cargoes to, from, and through New Orleans.

New Orleans, which is where it is because the Mississippi is where it is, is the undisputed home of another form of river music, Dixieland. Dixie, by the way, is an English corruption of the French word "dix" that appeared on the ten-dollar bank note of Louisiana before the Civil War. Cajun, now one of the more popular American foods, is another linguistic corruption. It is an Americanized form of Acadian, the eastern Canadian French-speaking people who were forced to flee Canada ten years before the American Revolution when they, too, refused to pledge allegiance to the British crown.

Louisiana, however, is not justly famous just for linguistic corruption but for politics as well. And old Earl Hingle knows about that. Earl was eighty-one last time we checked. Folks around his Delta town of Buras call him Mr. Earl, which doesn't mean he's a hairdresser. It's a Southern sign of respect.

For a very long time, politics in Louisiana meant the Democrats, not the party of Lincoln. Being a Democrat required no thought whatsoever. Any registered adult still breathing—and according to occasional comparisons of voter lists with tombstones, a good many who weren't—voted religiously and religiously voted Democratic. Technically, someone along the river in Louisiana could choose to be a Republican. But not many chose to. Times are changing across the South, however—even in Buras, where Earl's family now contains one Republican. That's Jody, his grandson. Jody is still allowed to vote, and the family clings to hope for his political redemption someday.

The economics and geography of the river are changing, too. For five thousand years the river has been lugging several thousand tons of dirt per day downriver and depositing it in the Delta, creating marshland and swampland, oddly shaped little islands spreading out into the Gulf, forming fertile freshwater fishing grounds. Along came settlers a couple of centuries ago. They fished and hunted in these marshlands and then, to make room for themselves and their houses, they began filling in the gaps between the odd islands. They even built a Louisiana state prison on one of these isolated, not-so-little accumulations of silt, using the river's vast volume of water and hidden currents as a most effective security moat.

Soon, the river, instead of spraying out widely, was confined for efficiency's sake to a broad channel of fresh water surrounded by marshes where salt water was increasingly creeping in, killing vegetation and eroding the Delta. Engineers are now trying to address this salt water encroachment by building river diversions to the north that steer a steady dose of fresh river water to flush through the endangered marshes.

Delta communities were not linked by road. The only link was water and boats. The eighty-foot freight boats came downriver once or twice a week from New Orleans, bringing supplies and ice in and taking cattle, oranges, fish, oysters, and shrimp out. Earl remembers making the noisy trips to New Orleans on deck with his mother and small herds of cows. Since Earl's daddy was an oysterman and a freight boat customer, the Hingle family rode the boat for free. Earl recalls, without contradiction from younger listeners, that the last boat was the *New Majestic* and its trips to New Orleans took ten hours. "It was fun to live at the time," he says, "but it's one of those things I wouldn't want to go back to."

Some modern conveniences like electricity and air-conditioning are dearly appreciated at least by those who knew life without them. "The lights and railroad came in late," Earl adds, "probably not till Eisenhower." That's how periods of time are often measured in these parts, by political eras. And exact years are remembered by their relationship to the worst hurricanes, as in "That was the year after Camille."

Earl runs, or rather, ran, an old-fashioned general store. Today, Earl's son Donald, who's sixty, runs the store, although his two brothers—Gerald and Calvin, the baby at fifty-two—are around frequently, too. Anywhere else such a store would likely be run by an ambitious new immigrant and the sign would call it a convenience store.

Hingle's still sells products that serve the convenience of its hardworking customers, such as sugar, ice, fishing gear, boots, of course, and hardware, nails, tools, and, naturally, gossip. There are no signs at Hingle's setting limits on the number of teenagers allowed inside at one time. No signs threatening police tows for vehicles parked too long beneath the towering shade trees out front. And no signs discouraging loitering. In fact, just as at Donald Gustafson's general store up at the river's Minnesota headwaters, riverfront customers at Hingle's way down in Louisiana are encouraged by a liberal coffee refill policy—and the air-conditioning—to linger, loiter, and, hopefully, gossip.

It could be effectively argued that gossiping—that is, two or more humans communicating with each other in person by using the spoken word to exchange stories and share opinions—is an essential grease to a properly functioning and civil society. Thanks to isolating phenomena such as long-distance telephones, faxes, E-mail, Sony Walkmans, and the like, genuine in-person communication has fallen on hard times. Can you imagine the look of shock and suspicion on most harried convenience store clerks these days if, during the crush of a typical morning's pay-in-advance-to-gas-up-and-get-your-first-shot-of-caffeine rush hour, one overtly friendly customer were to stall the impatient line at the cash register by casually standing there and saying, "So, what's new with you?"

It could also be effectively argued that investing that time in talking and listening, really listening, which is simply acknowledging the unspoken importance of the speaker, promotes a certain invaluable sense of well-being and belonging, that this shared life in general is moving along according to a comforting and civil if not always recognizable pattern.

The topics of discussion exchanged in such sessions are essentially irrelevant; it's the experience and the process that matter most. Traditionally, this process and experience occurred at general stores and post offices, on park benches and front porches, even around office water-coolers. Today, there's no time. Somehow, sitting on a park bench has become an open invitation to trouble from strangers. And anyway, park benches are either vandalized or in use by dissheveled sleepers. Front porches have been replaced by backyard decks surrounded for safety and privacy by fences and bushes. And what circumspect employee, in an era of corporate downsizing, wants to be seen idling anywhere, let alone around the water-cooler?

Without such personal interaction, the gossip void has been poorly filled by such things as 900 phone lines, rumor radio, celebrity journalism, and tabloid television, which together promote more outrage than openness, more cynicism than community. No wonder urban Americans so often feel painfully isolated!

But social serendipity seems to survive more easily along the river, especially in the South where the midday summer heat discourages unnecessary movement. Is it just my imagination or does it seem hotter when you leave an air-conditioned store today than it did in the old days Before Air-Conditioning when the store was just as hot, possibly even hotter, than outdoors?

Earl's old store was not air-conditioned. It was actually on the other side of the river in a town called Ostrica. See if you can follow this now, because it makes real sense in a place where a famous river is an everyday neighbor. Time was when people who lived in Buras on the west side of the river simply crossed the river like a broad boulevard to shop in Ostrica, to have a beer or three, to gossip, or to vote. When the road came in, however, it came down the west side into Buras. This eliminated the need for Ostrica. No one wanted to change for the longest time; they traveled over and back, over and back all the time. One of the last things to die in Ostrica was the community's Sunday night baseball game. Eventually, however, everyone including Earl moved over to Buras. Progress is inevitable in America.

Actually, Buras still has one resident, sometimes. He's Boshko Franicevich, who comes and goes, living in one aged structure near the water. He's tapped into a power source from somewhere, a frayed electric line that's drooping from a tilting pole. "When all the people lived here," Boshko says, "we had no power. Now, no one lives here and we've got power." It keeps his beer cool, runs the air-conditioner, and powers the old TV set that he leaves on all the time for company when he's in residence.

Thus Ostrica was in the unusual position of having no permanent residents except on election day when, under Louisiana law, fifty voters had to make the twenty-minute crossing back over from Buras to vote where they had originally registered to vote, at Earl's former general store, which was essentially abandoned. They still do this, by the way, though the number of voters has dwindled to thirty-three.

Ghost towns in semi-tropical regions look considerably different from ghost towns out west. Today, Ostrica, once a bustling little community where the *New Majestic* regularly docked and time was measured by the tides, looks more like a dense jungle where everything that doesn't move for a few minutes is quickly overgrown. When Mr. Earl waves his arm and says, "All the people lived over there," there is nothing there save for thick vines, dense weeds, and willowlike trees. In fact, without the sunken rotting boat and the crumbling landing, river passersby could easily overlook Ostrica completely. Its collection of buildings, barrels, piles of rusting bolts, and other abandoned community detritus is aging rapidly. And smells like it. Most of the dead community is hidden and overgrown by vegetation that thrives on the abundant moisture. Even Mr. Earl, weathered cane in hand, looks older as he strolls through Ostrica. He also has a pacemaker, an artificial knee, and a glass eye. "I've had a cough for a spell, too," he mentions. "I thought it passed me. Now it's coming back."

Still, Mr. Earl crosses the river regularly to combat the effects of rot, mildew, rust, wildlife, and wild plants on his old store, Hingle's Grocery and Bar, sitting so tidy on its soggy pilings. "In them days before The End," he says, "I also sold boat motors, Chrysler motors. The best. I had 'em in my boats, so I sold them, too, and the parts." He still paints the sprawling old structure every two years and regularly rents it out as a fishing camp to the likes of Wayne Stroupe, men from cities to the north who for a few days want to fish together, drink beer, not shower, sleep on suspicious mattresses, and get their drinking water from a barrel at the end of the rain gutter.

Water is everywhere in the Delta. Thoughtful neighbors post signs by their driveway: DON'T DRIVE IN WHEN WET. It's like living in a greenhouse atop a soggy sponge. There's water in the river right here, in the Gulf behind those trees, on your skin, coating any tiled surfaces, just beneath the soil. Even Buras's local church—Our Lady of Good Harbor—is named for water.

"Tide's coming in," Mr. Earl observes as he presses one foot into the squishy ground. "In the hurricanes," he remembers, "you'd have water up to that old gumball machine." There's so much water everywhere, even hanging in the humid air, that a new wire fence is crumbling rust within two years, though some suspect there's invisible chemicals floating downriver, too, that don't help the situation.

Cattle wander through the old town, grazing where they please on the flourishing free forage. Sometimes the heat seems to affect the livestock, causing them to walk into the river and stand up to their chins in water. It's cooling. More important, it prohibits the gajillions of mosquitoes from assaulting them quite so much. "I've seen mosquitoes so thick," Mr. Earl recalls, "they could kill a cow. They swarm in funnel-shaped clouds, hunting. When they hit town, we had to take inside, it was so bad." Some insects are good, however. Take the mud dauber wasps; please, take them. They feast on the Delta's spiders. "Oh, we got 'nough spiders around here," adds Mr. Earl. "That's for sure."

Then, with a surprising nautical nimbleness that tells of years of experience, Mr. Earl steps from Ostrica's crumbling landing down into Kenneth Fraderick's bouncing boat for the ride back home to Buras. Kenneth knows his boat and the rhythmic swells so well that he adjusts the engine and the tiller to hold the craft steady right next to, but not touching, the dock. "I could hold an egg between me and the dock," he says proudly, "without breaking the shell."

Kenneth's unnamed boat is 25 feet long, shorter than Jim Slavens's luxury boat and considerably less painted. Kenneth's boat bounces in the wake of an upbound ocean ship that passed by in mid-river five or six minutes before.

Kenneth is just back from another twelve-hour shrimp hunt in his boat. Instead of going to bed, he's relaxing by taking his boat out for fun. This is something else that makes sense along the Mississippi River. Kenneth left the Buras dock the previous night about six. His gray pants turned black with mosquitoes at that hour. He checked his gear, loaded a lunch pail of sandwiches and, perhaps, a bottle of his homemade peach brandy. Then he chugged across the darkening river, passed through the century-old locks that are really doors through the Mississippi riverbank out into the Gulf. His radio, tuned to one of those confoundingly cheery New Orleans commercial stations with its thirty-minute music sweeps, is played more for company than the popular music, news, and perpetually pessimistic traffic reports it sends out over Kenneth's nearby working world.

Shrimping is growing more difficult, Kenneth says, so much so that even his son has abandoned fishing for the security of a regular paycheck for work as a deckhand on a paraffin boat, a floating no-smoking zone. Kenneth has a litany of reasons for the difficulties of fishing. Shrimp season is closed in July and August and from December to May. The shrimp are smaller nowadays. Prices are down. Costs are up. A night's gas could set him back sixty dollars. Two new nets and associated gear cost eighteen hundred dollars. If he gets much more than one dollar per pound for a night's catch of less than a hundred pounds, he's happy. He goes for oysters at times, but oyster grounds are closed when the water gets high because of all the downbound pollution.

Then, of course, there are the Vietnamese. One

hears quite a bit of grumbling from old-timers about these newer newcomers. The criticism seems to focus on their being too good at fishing. They work hard and live close in clans. They overfish, it is said, and undersell. They also, of course, look different, and won't be found exchanging stories at the traditional places. And the Coast Guard, it is said, invests an inordinate amount of time and effort checking local boats for life preservers, flares, and garbage bags, and not near enough time monitoring the holds of foreign-born fishermen for overfishing.

Not far away, another boat, much larger at one hundred forty feet, is pulling away from the Mississippi's east bank for the quick crossing to the west. It's the combination passenger-car–ferry from Pointe a la Hache to West Pointe a la Hache. It's like a city bus, only free. People get on with their grocery bags, their bicycles, their cars and pickups and strollers. And twenty minutes or so later they get off on the other side, not one penny poorer. And it's better than driving forty miles north to the first bridge and then forty miles back down the other side.

Charles Ansardi takes the ferry at times, when he isn't herding livestock down the road to another pasture. Delta drivers simply wait for the herd to pass, as they would at a railroad crossing. Charles is a good-natured Delta cattleman who hates snakes. There are copperheads around and what they locally call Congos. They are black snakes, very mean and very poisonous. Everyone seems to know someone who's been bitten. The venom is actually the snake's gastric juices. They go to work right away digesting the victim from the inside out. So anyone who gets tagged by a Congo doesn't have long to get to the hospital. Charles returns the favor; he kills Congos on sight.

Also on the ferry at times is Roman Duplessis, a twenty-four-year-old unemployed oysterman who crosses from east to west for the cheaper groceries over there. "It's awful hard finding work around these parts," he says, sitting on the ferry bench. "But you survive, man, you survive. Hear what I'm saying?"

Also on the ferry much of the time are Bill Hingle, Alvin Williams, and Dale Fox. They're ferry pilots and crewmen. Billy has been crossing the Mississippi for twenty-five years, thirty-six times a day, back and forth and back and forth and back and forth. The ferryboat bridge is air-conditioned nowadays; some people might call it refrigerated.

"We never shut down," says Billy. "When the hurricanes come, we're the last thing running." He was a machinist for seven years up in New Orleans. But Delta people don't cotton too much to walls.

Billy remembers going catfishing pretty much every day in his youth. In those days a one-hundred-pound catfish was not extraordinary; today, a twenty-pounder is. "I wouldn't eat the fish outta this river now," says Billy, making a face and then winking. "Although it's easier to catch 'em now; most of 'em glow real good."

In Billy's youth the big banana boats would steam by upbound from Central America only a few hours from the city markets. The ships' crews would toss overboard large bunches of too-ripe bananas before the New Orleans buyers spotted them. Billy and his buddies would dive in and rescue the fruit for their families' tables and for possible quick sale to others.

Bill, Alvin, and Dale work seven days and seven nights, and then they have seven days off. "We're bayou people," says Alvin, "just trying to make ends meet and be outdoors in the fresh air and sun as much as possible. I think we're all born on boats."

Dale's got the river in his blood, too. His great-grandfather and his Uncle Henry were both ferry captains. They didn't earn the thirty-three-thousand-dollar salary Dale gets for captaining. But they were outside a lot. And although ferryboating has an approximate schedule, it allows its workers to feel more in control of their lives than, say, assembly line crews. Dale adjusts the air-conditioner to his preference, more like northern Canada than the Arctic. He brings with him a portable TV, for the frequent waits while loading, and a lunch pail with his dinner and ample fruit. While crossing the river, he also brings his own bottled water from home. "I wouldn't let my family drink this crap," he says. "You see everything going down this river. I mean everything. We used to swim in it. No more. And you see green scum on the rocks now."

The channel at Pointe a la Hache is about a hundred feet deep, even with the new rocks the Corps dumped in not so long ago to stabilize nearby banks. The only challenges, hurricanes aside, are the frequent winter fogs and the oceangoing ships, especially when the two come simultaneously. Dale even spends his days off in boats; he goes alligator hunting, now that it's legal again.

"Down here," he says, "you do whatever you can make a buck at." And he's got a daughter in college.

The river seems wider than it used to be to the veteran ferryboat workers. Also dirtier and busier. And their passengers seem a bit less friendly. Blacks and whites sit separately now, by choice, not racial fiat. Dale remembers playing with black children in his pre-integration childhood. "We shared toys," he says, "went swimming together. Now, no more. There's two worlds today."

Dale adjusts the ferry's throttle down to allow a small tanker to chug by downbound. The ship is owned by a Texan, registered in Panama, and carrying a cargo of fifteen different chemicals from the United States to Australia. At the helm is Charles Walton, one of about ninety men in a tight-knit fraternity of river navigators called the Crescent River Pilots Association.

These are the well-paid working descendants of the river pilots who arrived in the early 1700s to help steer ocean ships around the Mississippi River's countless navigational hazards. "I supposed," Mark Twain recalled years after his years as a river pilot, "that all a pilot had to do was keep his boat in the river and I did not consider that that could be much of a trick since it was so wide."

Charles Walton and his colleagues are paid considerably more than Twain—upwards of one hundred fifty thousand dollars a year for twenty-six weeks of round-the-clock duty shuttling the one hundred miles between New Orleans and a tiny, dying community called Pilottown near the Mississippi's mouth. These pilots invest nearly a decade of apprenticeship study, including endless hours watching the veterans and the river and at least one full year at sea, for the opportunity to be certified by the state as river pilots. A separate set of pilots specializes in guiding the ships the twenty-one miles between Pilottown and the open Gulf at the Southwest Pass seabuoy. In this last downbound stretch, the navigable river is about fifty feet deep, which leaves about thirty-six inches clearance for the larger ships.

Pilottown is a little-known piece of work. Once it was a bustling, if isolated, community of five hundred souls in well-kept little homes on raised foundations, all connected by elevated cement sidewalks that give mute but disturbing testimony to how high the water can get in a sea surge. The children in those days made the forty-mile watery round-trip commute to their Venice schools by boat.

Today, most of the homes are boarded up. The grocery has been shuttered for decades. And the nicest structure is the graceful old main house, a dormitory for on-duty pilots awaiting their next ride down or upriver. There is nowhere much to go from Pilottown, by land anyway. And no way to get there without a boat. The walkways all end out in the marshes, where many snakes live and some enterprising beekeepers have planted a few hives for the warmer months.

The pilots eat quite well, sleep comfortably, read on the extremely green lawn so carefully manicured by apprentices, or watch television. Although a wife or girlfriend passes through occasionally, Pilottown is a child-free society with one mascot, a five-foot wild alligator named Roy. He is friendly as alligators go, perhaps explained by the obvious overbite of his misaligned jaw, evidence of some long-ago altercation that made real hunting a challenge for him. So Pilottown's human residents care for their helpless lethal neighbor by twice a day tossing their table scraps off the elevated walkway in front of the house onto the muddy bottom beneath the long pier. A few water snakes slither away. Moments later, two bulbous eyes that were waiting, motionless, in the shallow water nearby, begin to move. Slowly, they glide through the water, and then out onto the mud waddles Roy, eager to consume his dinner before the next tide does.

Time was when communications along the riverbank consisted of cannons. Today, of course, there are radios, so pilots get a twenty-four-hour warning of approaching clients. They step out the front door and typically mount a bicycle for the three-minute ride past countless thumb-sized crabs that scurry out of the way down the long, narrow, and creaking pier to the shuttle boat out to the freighter.

It's a ten- to twelve-hour journey down from New Orleans to Pilottown and another three and a half hours out to the Southwest Pass seabuoy. Without pausing and usually without even noticing, the ships pass by—and above—communities like Pointe a la Hache, Buras and Ostrica, Port Sulphur and Empire, Triumph and Venice, the end of the road. On the east side, back in the overgrowth, sits Fort Saint Philip.

The crumbling old forgotten fort sits on a vital bend in the Mississippi where ships must slow for the turn. It was built there, not by accident, by the French in the 1750s. The

Spanish improved it later. But it did not see real military action until the War of 1812 when British ships sailing upriver to surprise General Andrew Jackson's American troops at New Orleans began a nine-day bombardment. Every two minutes a shell fell on the fort. But the fort held. And so did General Jackson's military reputation, enabling him, like Generals Grant and Eisenhower later, to move on to the presidency. Then, in 1862 Admiral David Farragut led a Union fleet upriver and conquered Southern forces there. His victory shut off the Confederacy's maritime back door.

Today the fort is privately owned by Frank Ashby, a Louisiana oilman whose fortune is insufficient to restore the place for anything other than a fishing camp and as an historical oddity for tourists who can afford an expensive helicopter or boat ride. But Frank knew how special this overgrown outpost of history was to his father; Frank had his father's ashes spread there.

Below the fort now, fifteen to twenty times every day, the Pilottown shuttle boat speeds out into the river, matching its course and speed to another oceangoing vessel. Slowly, they get closer and closer alongside until Charles Walton leaps off the outbound tanker. Alan Diamond or one of the other pilots leaps aboard to pilot the next leg. And the two ships diverge.

Their mutual swells catch Berlin Moreau's inbound boat, the twenty-eight-foot *Po Boy*. Berlin is a fisherman, the grandson and son of fishermen, and the father and grandfather of more fishermen. In fact, all three of Berlin's boys make a living fishing, or try to. On this day, Berlin took one hundred forty pounds of fish from these waters, mostly pollock, which he sold to P & L Seafoods in Venice for ninety cents a pound. He also caught one small shark, which brings only twenty cents a pound for its meat but twelve dollars a pound for its fins.

It's tough to support a family on such short income from such long days. Hard physical labor, especially extracting natural resources such as commercial fishing, mining, and logging, is having a hard time surviving as a viable occupation in the United States of the late twentieth century. That's "Progress," although the transition has trapped a generation of would-be workers like Berlin's boys, who withdrew from high school to prepare for one career and now find their opportunities withering. Now, it seems, workers must pay a price to do what their daddies did well and what they, too, are good at. Berlin tried carpentering a while up in Baton Rouge. There is a psychic satisfaction that accompanies working hard with your hands all day and having something in them to show for it at quitting time. You don't get that feeling from composing E-mail messages. "I had to come back to the river," Berlin says. "I'm happy when my feet hit the deck. I'm my own boss out here. You go where you want, come and go when you want. It's a good life, a hard life, but a good life."

He takes a deep breath of the brisk salt air blowing inland in the deepening darkness of another clear summer night. He feels the fiberglass boat bang into the invisible swells beneath the *Po Boy*, its two-hundred-ten-horsepower diesel throbbing below deck, and heads the last thirty-one miles for home. Hopefully, there is nothing large and hard drifting downriver in these same swells.

To the inexperienced eye, the lower

Berlin Moreau, Claude Gerkin, Russell Stanbey (*left to right*), following the shrimp to the Gulf of Mexico

Mississippi River at night looks empty and black, more like a vast, motionless lake whose distant shoreline is inhabited by surprisingly few lights. But Berlin, his head constantly turning this way and that like an alert owl's, can sniff the winds, monitor the motor's moods, and decipher the lights that are there, differentiating the buoys and boats from towns and reading the stars' visibility for tomorrow's weather. He'll never get on the evening news for such skills. But he feels good about them and about having accumulated them over so many years in the same stretch of the Mississippi River, like his father and grandfather before him.

Even in the broad river's dense darkness the fifty-three-year-old Berlin could find any of the dozen passes out to sea, as if they were in his own house and he were shuffling through the darkness in his slippers. And Berlin would also know which passes would most likely give up a profitable harvest at this time of day and at this time of year. Shortly before midnight, Berlin eases the *Po Boy* into her berth in the darkness. He ties the familiar knot in the lines, the one he's tied countless thousands of times as a tidy, proud punctuation mark to one more workday on the mighty Mississippi. Then he smiles.

Davey Johnson smiles, too. He's flicking switches, reading seventeen gauges, resetting dials. He looks to the right. He looks to the left. "Clear!" he yells. And the whine begins.

Soft at first. Then, building in volume, the turbine goes to work. Fifteen seconds later, the huge blades above begin their first swing of the day, slowly at first and then gradually gaining in speed until, surely, the blurred blades can go no faster. But

Davey Johnson, pilot for Evergreen International Helicopters, Inc., Venice, Louisiana

they are just warming up.

Davey Johnson and his helicopter are about to take off again. As Berlin Moreau lives for the hours his feet are on a deck, Davey lives for his moments of flight. "All right, everyone," the pilot announces. "Let's remember, as we cruise the friendly skies of Louisiana this morning, that the most important thing if we go down is, 'Get the pilot out!' Got that?"

Davey Johnson grew up in Lexie, Mississippi, the product of a mixed marriage—a Southern father and Yankee mother. As a youngster in the informal backyards of Lexie, little Davey would shuck off his socks out of his mother's sight and look up into the big Southern sky most days. There, he'd surely spot another airplane silently making its way through the clouds at heights the little boy could not imagine. The youngster would wonder how those heavy machines could move so gracefully and quickly, who was in them, and where they were going.

Now he knows. Davey Johnson is in his forties. He's been flying all kinds of airplanes for nearly half his life, ever since that day in the Army when he jumped into the medical examination line for pilots. In those days military pilots, especially helicopter pilots, had one destination: Vietnam. So Davey Johnson spent three hundred ninety-seven days there, not that anyone was counting, flying fresh troops into dangerous places and broken men out to safe places. He also flew low, real low in a scout chopper, so that other people he never saw would see him and shoot at him. This, then, would attract the armed attention of Davey's larger, heavier chopper colleagues, flying above and behind him. That's the way it worked in theory anyway. "I found," Davey recalls, "that you live life fully at two hundred feet with bullets flying by in the opposite direction. It does tend to keep your blood moving."

Davey is wearing his own flying uniform now—blue jeans, neat short-sleeved shirt with epaulets and flapped pockets, a company baseball cap, standard pilot sunglasses, and sandals. "I hate socks," he says. "I only wear them when my mother is around."

Davey Johnson favors helicopters above all planes. "Some planes want to fly themselves," he explains. "A chopper now, you let it go and it wants to turn upside down. Not my idea of flying." And he delights in the freedom that comes with helicopter flying, like riding a motorcycle or waterskiing outside the wake. "In a fixed wing plane," he says, "you take off and you know you want to go to another airport and land in a straight line. And if you change your mind about that, you can get in a bind right quick. In a chopper you go where you want how you want."

As soon as he enters his flying world, the moustachioed Davey removes the company baseball cap and dons his campaign hat, that camouflage-colored, floppy-brimmed cowboy hat that carried him safely through the skies of Southeast Asia. "You gotta have a trademark for people to talk about, right?" He winks. Then he's ready.

"You boys ready to go flyin'?" he asks.

Now that he hears the engine running properly, confirming the gauges, Davey pulls a pair of bulbous headphones down over his head and hat and adjusts the voice-activated microphone so it barely touches his lips. He twists the throttle. Suddenly the blades begin whirling overhead even faster, five times every second.

The chopper is shaking and jumping now, like an eager sled dog pulling at the reins ready to run. Davey tightens his seat harness. He pulls up with his left hand. The craft shakes harder. It breaks free of the ground. Then it sinks suddenly, slightly to the rear. Davey smiles across the cockpit. His tanned feet are moving ever so gently. The chopper turns in place. The plane moves ahead now, slowly, level, across an empty field, destroying a cloud of unsuspecting mosquitoes and always avoiding wires. Then it breaks to the left and shoots straight up, suddenly soaring out over the darkness of an adjacent swamp. Davey is humming into his microphone.

The ground quickly falls away below, far below. The modest lights of Venice, Louisiana, disappear to the rear. Davey is in his element now. Let some other little boys in unseen backyards below look up at the sound of a flying machine and wonder at the speed and grace of Davey Johnson. "Louisiana," he says, "looks a lot like Vietnam without the tracers."

Davey flies helicopter charters out of Venice most days. He takes virtually anything anywhere, though he shies away from the herbicide flights with federal narcotics agents spraying isolated marijuana patches. Much of his time is invested in servicing the brigade of oil rigs that stand so lonely and tall way out in the Gulf. He points to a few distant dots of lights twinkling on the horizon. Each one needs new crews, milk, cereal, mail, and rig parts. "I'll show you small," Davey says. "Small is a four seat helicopter one hundred miles off the mouth of this mammoth river looking for a little ole oil rig. That's small."

That explains Davey's careful calculations before each flight, figuring the weight of the plane and its cargo, including himself. That also explains Davey Johnson's flying credo: "'Tis better to have a fuel reserve than not."

It's a tad brisk in the predawn moments in Davey's unheated chopper, what with the one hundred fifty-mile-an-hour downdraft from the blades blasting by the door, which has been removed for visibility. That passing chill may, in fact, be the worst thing about the life of Davey Johnson, hater of all things cold. "I don't do winters well," he says. "The way I look at it, you don't get snow without it being thirty-two degrees cold, which is about sixty fewer than I like. So I don't intend to ever go much farther north than right here."

Except for the monthly visits to his wife, Dee, and their family, Jennifer, who is twelve going on twenty, and Joey, the four-year-old who earned his nickname of Cujo by kicking the dryer one day and breaking his foot. He might be a chopper pilot in the making.

Despite all his hours in the air, Davey's enthusiasm for the world of flying never seems to wane. He'll take his chopper down just above the trees and blast across the swamps for a few miles, reveling in the freedom and sense of speed, spotting startled animals dashing away, nutria leaping into the water, and alligators slithering from the banks. He'll pass over old Fort Saint Philip and speculate about the battles there. He'll spot the tell-tale ripples of a school of passionate redfish spawning. And he'll marvel at the Mississippi flowing steadily by and the Army Corps of Engineers' imaginative engineering efforts to steer and tame the river by keeping it busy with itself.

"The scale of this place is marvelous, isn't it? But listen to me. They're not going to stop this ole river from going where it wants to go."

Davey flicks on the radio. Aeronautical protocol, like river manners, requires him to announce his presence. A voice comes back in his earphones. "Well, g'morning, David. You up early, guy."

It's Jeff Jones at a nearby airfield. Davey recognizes his voice. They're radio friends, though Davey is unlikely to spot Jeff in a crowd. "We is immortalizing the river this mornin'," Davey says. On the left is the tiny light cluster of Pilottown. Down there, it's still darkness. But up at one thousand feet the first glimmers of dawn are appearing to the east over Florida.

Then Davey points to a mid-river white wake ahead. It's the *Atlantic Dreamer*, a rusty freighter out of Monrovia, only a few miles from dropping off its last pilot and entering the Gulf, where so many German U-boats lurked a half century before. "The river is busy pretty much twenty-four hours a day," Davey notes.

Indeed, Berlin Moreau is untying the *Po Boy* again right about now as an informal squadron of pleasure boats races downriver for a full day of fishing beneath the brutal sun. Maybe thirty miles to the north the air-conditioner on the ferry at Pointe a la Hache is warming up to chill down the bridge for another day of river crossings, while Earl Hingle enjoys retirement by sleeping in some more.

Ninety miles farther upstream and they're still gambling in the new New Orleans casinos. In Vicksburg, the scale-model Mississippi is still flowing and Tom Pokrefke is still studying its mysterious hydraulics, while Roger Saucier plots his retirement—near the river, of course.

The Federal Express terminal is quiet by now, but Leland Olivier's dredging crew grinds on through the muck by Hickman, Kentucky. Just off Cairo, 953.8 river miles above the Mississippi's mighty mouth, Sandy Padgett is cooking up another hearty breakfast for the *Sumac*'s crew before another long workday. Jim Slavens's boat floats peacefully in Davenport while he dresses for his short commute to the bank and the *President* prepares for another breakfast gambling cruise.

In Wisconsin, Aloysius, Fred, Chester, and the Anderson House's other rent-a-cats in Wabasha are returning to their own room overlooking the river to dine on some welcome cat food they think smells delicious. The commuter traffic will soon be building all over the Twin Cities. While up at Lake Itasca, nearly twenty-four hundred miles from Davey's chopper, the deer are retreating as a few hundred slightly stiff campers stir in their sleeping bags. The aroma of fresh-brewed coffee fills the Gustafsons' general store and in the nearby woods, piney-wet with dew, a few more gallons of lake water trickle past the headwater's stones to start their trek.

Right on time, Davey Johnson's chopper arrives at the bottom of the Mississippi River, far beyond the end of roads. There the craft hovers, whop-whopping to bear noisy witness to the natural finale being unveiled several hundred feet below in the empty river. Slowly, like a new black and white photograph emerging from within a tank of developing chemicals, daylight creeps across the Delta. It reveals twin thin strips of soil, transplanted grain by grain from far to the north, delicately denoting the river's banks far out into the salt water. In between, looking far too strong to be hemmed in by such fragile walls, the massive Mississippi River moves on, its mighty work nearly complete for this journey.

In its ponderous journey from those first clear moments jostling so crisply and innocently around the stepping-stones at the end of Lake Itasca, the river has flowed more than 12.3 million feet and collected the water, the goods, and the refuse of the Ohio and Missouri Rivers, which together flow even farther. The Mississippi has carried thousands of boats and barges and people and upwards of a half billion tons of man-made cargo, plus thousands of tons more silt. It has entertained, awed, and soothed. It has provided food for tables and food for thought, relaxation, scenery, company, and comfort. And it has destroyed some dreams as well.

Its waters move slower now; the incline is less. And with its cargoes of dirt, trees, limbs, chemicals, and other urban discards headed for the invisible fathoms of the Gulf's depths, the Mississippi River looks perhaps tired, certainly darker, than the surrounding blue tropical sea as far out as the eye can see.

And then, when the sun finally fully squeezes above the watery horizon, a perfect circle all orange and bright and full of promise, the air over the river warms immediately. Davey's sandaled feet work the pedals and his hand the throttle to hold the craft steady and still for this spectacle. The radio and a trio of spectators are silent, out of respect.

Down below, without stop, the mighty Mississippi River joins fifteen million of its muddy gallons with the sea every second. Its long, momentous journey ends silently and unnoticed, just as that first single snowflake fell so silently and unseen in northern Canada so far away and so long ago.

And the Mississippi River flows on, as it has here now for some forty-eight million other dawns just like this one.